Foreword

*A*ssessing Student Outcomes: Performance Assessment Using the Dimensions of Learning Model is both a welcome response to the revolution in assessment now under way in American education and a welcome addition to the Dimensions of Learning materials introduced by ASCD in 1992. The Dimensions of Learning instructional model is based on the premise that fives types of thinking are essential to the learning process: (1) positive attitudes and perceptions about learning, (2) thinking involved in acquiring and integrating knowledge, (3) thinking involved in extending and refining knowledge, (4) thinking involved in using knowledge meaningfully, and (5) productive habits of mind. The authors have used this instructional model to develop a practical approach to student assessment that answers many of the recent demands for reform in this area. For instance, they address the need for educators to specify not only the content-specific knowledge and skills students should acquire, but also the knowledge and skills that cut across many content areas and are useful to people in many situations during their lifetime.

What is most refreshing about this book is the authors' recognition of the connections among teaching, learning, and assessment. Rather than view assessment as a separate activity, they closely link it to teaching and learning and suggest that it be conducted in a manner that provides useful feedback to teachers, students, parents, and others interested in real student achievement. Central to their approach is the use of carefully constructed performance tasks that give students opportunities to demonstrate their understanding of concepts and apply knowledge and skills as they would in the world outside of school. Teachers will find the authors' guidelines for developing performance tasks especially valuable.

The *rubrics* for assessing performance are another important and unique element of this approach to assessment. As defined by the authors, a rubric consists of descriptions of four levels of performance for a given standard, each of which is assigned a score ranging from a low of 1 to a high of 4. The authors have included numerous rubrics for both teachers and students that can be adapted for use in the classroom.

The approach to assessment described in this book, supported as it is by an established instructional model, will undoubtedly help teachers develop more effective assessments that are strongly linked to teaching and learning. And by changing the way they look at student assessment, teachers will be taking a big step toward transforming their classrooms into places where we know that students will experience learning to the fullest and acquire the knowledge and skills necessary to be vital, contributing members of society.

BARBARA TALBERT JACKSON
ASCD President, 1993-94

Assessing Student Outcomes

Performance Assessment
Using the Dimensions of Learning Model

Robert J. Marzano

Debra J. Pickering

Jay McTighe

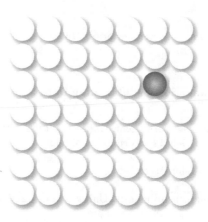

Association for Supervision and Curriculum Development
Alexandria, Virginia USA

Association for Supervision and Curriculum Development
1703 N. Beauregard St. • Alexandria, VA 22311-1714 USA
Telephone: 1-800-933-2723 or 703-578-9600 • Fax: 703-575-5400
Web site: http://www.ascd.org • E-mail: member@ascd.org

Printed in the United States of America.

Typeset by Valerie Sprague

Stock no. 61193179
ASCD member price: $13.95   nonmember price: $16.95

Library of Congress Cataloging-in-Publication Data

Marzano, Robert J.
    Assessing student outcomes : performance assessment using the dimensions of learning
  model / Robert J. Marzano, Debra Pickering, Jay McTighe.
      p.   cm.
    Includes bibliographical references.
    ISBN 0-87120-225-5
    1. Educational tests and measurements—United States. 2. Grading and marking
  (Students)—United States. I. Pickering, Debra.
  II. McTighe, Jay. III. Title.
  LB3051.M457   1994
  371.2′6′0973—dc20   93-41882
                                                                          CIP

04 03 02 01   10 9 8 7 6

Assessing Student Outcomes

Performance Assessment Using the Dimensions of Learning Model

Introduction

Dimensions of Learning is an instructional framework based on the best of what research and theory say about learning. Its premise is that five types of thinking, what we call the five dimensions of learning, are essential to successful learning. Initially, Dimensions of Learning was designed to help teachers better plan curriculum and instruction by using what is known about how students learn. The framework's strong grounding in research and theory, however, makes it a natural partner for performance assessment. Dimensions of Learning and performance assessment share similar assumptions about the nature of learning and the art and science of teaching. In fact, we believe Dimensions of Learning can help educators answer one of the most frequently asked questions concerning performance assessment: How do you teach to performance assessment? In this book, we describe how to design a performance assessment system that supports the Dimensions of Learning instructional framework.

The next section briefly describes the five dimensions of learning and how they work together. Readers who would like a more thorough grounding in the theory and use of the Dimensions of Learning framework may want to examine one or more of the following publications:

• The *Dimensions of Learning Teacher's Manual* (Marzano et al. 1992a) describes how to teach using the Dimensions of Learning framework.

• The *Dimensions of Learning Trainer's Manual* (Marzano et al. 1992b) provides a step-by-step guide to training teachers in the use of the framework. It is designed to be used with the *Teacher's Manual.*

• *A Different Kind of Classroom: Teaching with Dimensions of Learning* (Marzano 1992) describes the theoretical underpinnings of the Dimensions of Learning framework and provides examples of how teachers can use the framework to plan lessons.

The Five Dimensions of Learning

Before describing how to approach performance assessment using Dimensions of Learning, let's briefly consider the framework itself. What are the five dimensions of learning, and what do they imply about effective instruction?

Dimension 1: Positive Attitudes and Perceptions About Learning

Without positive attitudes and perceptions, students have little chance of learning proficiently, if at all. In other words, for learning to occur, students must have certain attitudes and perceptions. Feeling comfortable in the classroom, for instance, is important to learning. If a student does not believe the classroom is a safe and orderly place, she will probably learn little in that classroom. Similarly, if she does not have positive attitudes about classroom tasks, she probably won't put much effort into them and, again, her learning will suffer. A primary focus of effective instruction, then, is establishing positive attitudes and perceptions about learning.

Dimension 2: Acquiring and Integrating Knowledge

Helping students acquire new knowledge, integrate it with what they already know, and retain it is an important aspect of learning. When content is new, a teacher's instructional planning must focus on strategies that will help students relate new knowledge to prior knowledge, organize the new knowledge in meaningful ways, and make it part of their long-term memory. For example, a teacher might help students relate the new information they are learning to what they already know by helping them create an analogy for the new information. He might suggest that they construct an outline or a graphic representation of the new information. And he might help students more effectively store information in long-term memory by guiding them through the creation of images representing the important aspects of the new information.

The *Dimensions of Learning Teacher's Manual* outlines numerous instructional strategies teachers can use to help students acquire and integrate knowledge more effectively.

Dimension 3: Extending and Refining Knowledge

Acquiring and integrating knowledge is not the end of the learning process. Learners extend and refine their knowledge, adding new distinctions and making further connections. They analyze what they have learned in more depth and with more rigor. While extending and refining their knowledge, learners commonly engage in the following activities:

- Comparing
- Classifying
- Making inductions
- Making deductions
- Analyzing errors
- Creating and analyzing support
- Analyzing perspectives
- Abstracting

Teachers need to consider two important planning questions when addressing Dimension 3:

- What information is important for students to extend and refine?
- What strategies and activities will be used to help students extend and refine their knowledge?

The kinds of extending and refining activities chosen should fit naturally with the curriculum content, so as to fully integrate the teaching of cognitive skills and the teaching of content. Again, the *Dimensions of Learning Teacher's Manual* provides numerous examples, at both the elementary and secondary level, of strategies and activities that help students master each of the eight extending and refining skills.

Dimension 4: Using Knowledge Meaningfully

Cognitive psychologists tell us that the most effective learning occurs when students are able to use knowledge to perform meaningful tasks. For instance, you might initially learn about good used cars by talking to a friend or reading an article about them. You really learn about them, though, when you have to decide which car to buy on your limited budget. In effect, the "meaningful task" of making a decision provides an arena for you to learn about cars at a much deeper and richer level than you would if you weren't involved in the task. Planning instruction so that students have the opportunity to use knowledge meaningfully is one of the most important decisions a teacher can make. In the Dimensions of Learning model, there are five types of tasks that encourage the meaningful use of knowledge:

- Decision making
- Investigation
- Experimental inquiry
- Problem solving
- Invention

A teacher should look at the content for significant issues or problems that naturally stand out. The content should determine which of the five tasks a teacher or student might select, not vice versa. Here are a few questions a teacher might think about to identify significant issues for the task of investigation:

• Is there an unresolved issue about how something occurred or why it occurred? (historical investigation)
• Is there an unresolved issue about what would happen if . . . or what would have happened if . . . ? (projective investigation)
• How many issues will be considered?
• Who will structure the tasks? (Ultimately, students should identify the issues they want to deal with in their projects and the specifics of those tasks; however, teachers must usually first provide structured activities to help students learn how to identify and carry out the five Dimension 4 activities.)
• What types of products will students produce?
• To what extent will students work in cooperative groups?

The *Dimensions of Learning Teacher's Manual* contains numerous examples of meaningful-use tasks that both elementary and secondary students might carry out.

Dimension 5: Productive Habits of Mind

The final aspect of learning is perhaps the most important. It concerns the use of productive habits of mind—habits used by critical, creative, and self-regulated thinkers. Although acquiring content knowledge is important, it is perhaps not the most important goal of education. Ultimately, developing mental habits that will enable individuals to learn on their own whatever they want or need to know at any point in their lives is probably the most important goal of education. Some of these habits of mind include:

• Being clear and seeking clarity
• Being open-minded

• Restraining impulsivity
• Being aware of your own thinking
• Evaluating the effectiveness of your actions
• Pushing the limits of your knowledge and abilities
• Engaging intensely in tasks even when answers or solutions are not immediately apparent

When teachers plan lessons, they often do not consciously consider activities or strategies they might use to help students develop productive habits of mind. They focus instead on content and on the need to "cover the curriculum." The Dimensions of Learning model specifies that teachers should consider in their planning questions that focus on developing productive habits of mind:

• Which mental habits should be emphasized in this unit?
• Which mental habits will be introduced?
• How will the mental habits be reinforced?

A complete explanation of the questions teachers should consider when planning a unit of instruction that addresses all five dimensions of learning can be found in *A Different Kind of Classroom: Teaching with Dimensions of Learning* and in the *Dimensions of Learning Teacher's Manual.*

The Relationship Among the Dimensions of Learning

It's important to realize that the five dimensions of learning do not operate in isolation but work together in the manner depicted in Figure 1. Briefly, Figure 1 illustrates that all learning takes place against the backdrop of the learner's attitudes and perceptions (Dimension 1) and her use (or lack of use) of the productive habits of mind (Dimension 5). If a student has negative attitudes and perceptions about learning, then she will likely learn little. If she has positive attitudes and perceptions, she will learn more, and learning will be easier. Similarly, when a student uses productive habits of mind, she fa-

FIGURE 1
Dimensions of Learning

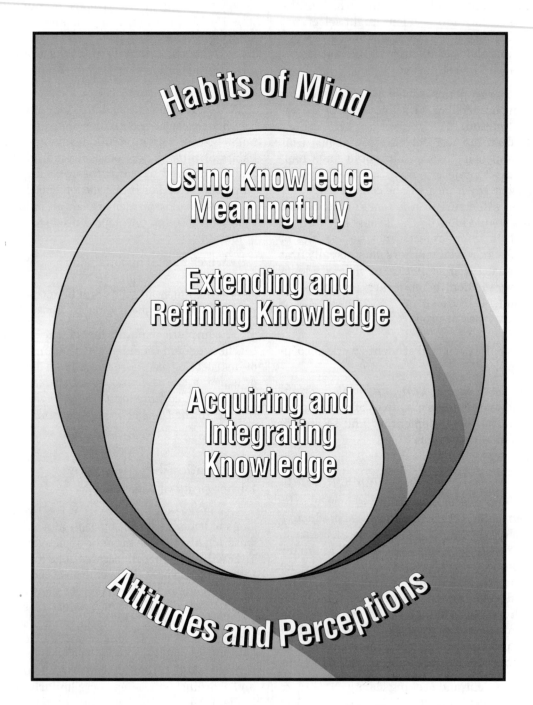

cilitates her learning; when she doesn't use productive habits of mind, she hinders her learning. Dimensions 1 and 5, then, are always factors in the learning process. This is why they are part of the background of Figure 1.

Given that proper attitudes and perceptions are in place and productive habits of mind are being used, learning is a matter of acquiring and integrating new knowledge (Dimension 2). Usually, though, the learner extends and refines knowledge as he acquires and integrates it. This is why the circle representing Dimension 2 overlaps the circle representing Dimension 3. While these two types of learning are going on, the learner should also be using knowledge meaningfully (Dimension 4)—applying his knowledge to round out the learning process.

The most effective learning is a product of the interaction of these five distinct types of thinking that we call the dimensions of learning.

The Importance of Understanding the Dimensions of Learning Model

Even this brief description of the Dimensions of Learning model implies some significant changes in the nature and function of schooling. For example, if we want students to engage in complex tasks in which they will use knowledge in unique and meaningful ways (Dimension 4) and if we want them to cultivate such higher level mental skills as restraining impulsivity and being aware of their own thinking (Dimension 5), then our methods of assessment must surely change, because most of today's assessments make no attempt to measure such behaviors; they are not linked to the kind of learning we want to see. Likewise, the nature and delivery of curriculum must also change to become more strongly linked to learning and assessment. Indeed, a primary purpose of this book is to illustrate how both assessment and curriculum must change if a school or district truly wishes to institutionalize the principles of Dimensions of Learning.

This brief discussion of Dimensions of Learning should provide you with the understanding necessary to make good use of this book. To get the most from the book, however, we encourage you to become thoroughly familiar with the model by reading *A Different Kind of Classroom: Teaching with Dimensions of Learning.*

Part One
A Discussion of Assessment

1

The Changing Face of Educational Assessment

The last decade has witnessed a growing recognition of the need for significant changes in educational assessment practices (Archbald and Newmann 1988, Shepard 1989). The calls for reform are directed not only at large-scale, standardized tests but also at classroom assessment practices. At least three factors have contributed to the demands for assessment reform: the changing nature of educational goals; the relationship between assessment and teaching and learning; and the limitations of the current methods of recording performance and reporting credit.

The Changing Nature of Educational Goals

The "back to basics" movement of the 1970s led to an emphasis on low-level functional skills and the proliferation of minimum-competency tests. The reform movement of the 1990s, however, is directed toward more sophisticated educational goals and higher standards. This new emphasis is perhaps most publicly symbolized by the 1991 "education summit" in Charlottesville, Virginia, during which President Bush and the nation's state governors presented America 2000, a proposal outlining an ambitious set of national education goals targeted for the year 2000 (Bush 1991). America 2000 called for no less

than the best schools in the world, schools that will enable all students to meet "world class" academic standards. In response, subject-area associations and commissioned groups began charting a set of national curriculum standards to provide greater specificity about what students should know and be able to do in each of the content areas.

Educators, legislators, business leaders, and parents recognize that educational goals should reach far beyond the scope of traditional subject-area domains. For example, in the report *What Work Requires of Schools* (Secretary's Commission 1991), the Department of Labor identifies a broad array of both academic and nonacademic competencies as necessary for the modern workplace, including:

- creative thinking
- decision making
- problem solving
- learning how to learn
- collaboration
- self-management

This emphasis on goals outside the traditional content disciplines is also reflected in some popular approaches to school reform not necessarily associated with the America 2000 proposal or its related efforts. For example, William Spady, an advocate of outcome-based education, argues persuasively that educators must broaden their target to include outcomes that relate to lifelong learning (Spady 1988).

Given these recommendations, many districts, and even entire states, have focused their attention on identifying important "exit outcomes" or "learner outcomes." For example, the Aurora Public Schools in Aurora, Colorado, have identified five lifelong learning outcomes and their related proficiencies (Redding 1991):

Outcome 1: A Self-Directed Learner
- Sets priorities and achievable goals
- Monitors and evaluates progress
- Creates options for self
- Assumes responsibility for actions
- Creates a positive vision for self

Outcome 2: A Collaborative Worker
- Monitors own behavior as a group member
- Assesses and manages group functioning
- Demonstrates interactive communication
- Demonstrates consideration for individual differences

Outcome 3: A Complex Thinker
- Uses a wide variety of strategies for managing complex issues
- Selects strategies appropriate to the resolution of complex issues and applies the strategies with accuracy and thoroughness
- Accesses and uses topic-relevant knowledge

Outcome 4: A Quality Producer
- Creates products that achieve their purpose
- Creates products appropriate to their intended audience
- Creates products that reflect craftsmanship
- Uses appropriate resources/technology

Outcome 5: Community Contributor
- Demonstrates knowledge about his or her diverse communities
- Takes action
- Reflects on role as a community contributor

Similarly, the state of Kentucky has identified six broad learning goals as the foundation for its ambitious educational reform agenda (Kentucky Department of Education 1991). These learning goals for students combine traditional academic outcomes with lifelong competencies necessary for success beyond the schoolhouse walls:

Goal 1: Apply basic communication and mathematics skills in situations similar to what they will experience in life

Goal 2: Apply core concepts and principles from mathematics, science, social studies, arts, and practical living studies, and vocational studies to situations similar to what they will experience in life

Goal 3: Demonstrate self-sufficiency

Goal 4: Demonstrate responsible citizenship

Goal 5: Think and solve problems

Goal 6: Integrate knowledge across disciplines

A number of other states, including Maine, Michigan, Minnesota, Pennsylvania, and Virginia, have included similar lifelong learning outcomes among their revised educational goals.

In short, educators are increasingly seeing the need to identify standards for both traditional discipline knowledge and outcomes that relate to lifelong learning. Although educators have acknowledged the importance of reinforcing standards and outcomes like those listed above, they have quickly recognized that current assessments do not adequately address these standards and outcomes. For the most part, standardized tests require students to recall or recognize fragmented and isolated bits of information. They rarely ask students to apply that information, and they almost never require students to exhibit proficiencies in the "higher forms" of cognition, such as complex reasoning and self-directedness (Marzano and Costa 1988). Lauren Resnick characterizes the problem in this way:

Many of the tests we do use are unable to measure what should be the hallmark of a "thinking" curriculum: the cultivation of students' ability to apply skills and knowledge to real-world problems. Testing practices may in fact interfere with the kind of higher order skills that are desired (Resnick 1987, p. 47).

These shortcomings make it clear that new approaches to assessment are needed if we are to satisfactorily assess students' ability to meet the lifelong learning standards and demanding content standards and outcomes that are the centerpiece of the plan to make the American public education system the best in the world.

The Relationship Between Assessment and Teaching and Learning

A second factor contributing to the need for assessment reform involves the relationship between assessment and the processes of teaching and learning. Behavioral theories that characterize learning as the accumulation of discrete skills have given way to a conception of learning and teaching based on cognitive psychology. Lori Shepard summarizes this shifting conception of the learning process:

> The notion that learning comes about by the accretion of little bits is outmoded learning theory. Current models of learning based on cognitive psychology contend that learners gain understanding when they construct their own knowledge and develop their own cognitive maps of the interconnections among facts and concepts . . . . Real learning cannot be spoon-fed one skill at a time (Shepard 1989, pp. 5-6).

As Shepard's comments imply, this cognitive view calls for an active, constructive approach to learning in which the whole is greater than the sum of the parts. This holistic view of learning is reflected in contemporary instructional methods such as integrated language arts; "hands-on, minds-on" approaches in science; writing-to-learn across the curriculum; problem solving and reasoning emphases in mathematics; and cooperative learning. If learning occurs in a holistic fashion, then assessments, too, should be able to provide holistic information, not just bits of information. This shift in emphasis is made explicit in a report from the National Commission on Testing and Public Policy:

> If we want students to learn how to solve open-ended science problems, we should assess their problem-solving skills by other means than multiple-choice tests in which they choose among alternative prescribed answers. Carefully crafted assessments would ask students to supply answers, perform observable acts, demonstrate skills, create products, and supply portfolios of work (National Commission on Testing and Public Policy 1991).

Conventional selected-response test formats (e.g., multiple choice, true/false, matching) are quite narrow in their focus. They provide only a snapshot or a "one moment in time" picture of learning. Although such sampling may have certain uses, it is generally incapable of revealing in any comprehensive way what students know and can do. Moreover, the conditions of such tests are often highly controlled. Students complete the work within inflexible time limits and have restricted access to resources and limited opportunities to make revisions. These kinds of tests also sacrifice authenticity, since they differ markedly from the ways in which people apply knowledge in the world outside of school. Despite these limitations, the results of such one-time measures are frequently used to make significant decisions, such as whether a student should be admitted to or excluded from special programs and what final grade a student will receive in a class.

What we now know about learning indicates that assessment and learning are closely and intimately tied. The importance of changing assessment practices so they mirror the learning process becomes more clear when one realizes that students in American schools learn what they know they will be tested on. This behavior was dramatically brought to the public's attention in 1983 in Walter Doyle's commissioned paper for the now-famous report *A Nation At Risk* (National Commission on Excellence in Education 1983). Doyle found that students in American schools soon discover that all things learned are not equal: you are tested on some and not on others. Not surprisingly, most students choose to ignore those things on which they are not tested. And teachers tend to consciously or unconsciously focus their instruction on the learnings that are prescribed and tested by the school, district, or state (Doyle 1983). In effect, then, assessment has both a direct and an indirect effect on learning. Assessment directly affects learning in that it provides the necessary feedback for effective learning. It indirectly affects learning in that instruction is commonly skewed toward what is assessed; and, obviously, what is taught affects what is learned.

Given our new understanding of the learning process and the relationship between assessment and both teaching and learning, there is little doubt that reformed assessment practices are long overdue.

The Limitations of the Present Ways of Recording Student Performance and Reporting Credit

A third factor driving assessment reform is the manner in which achievement data are recorded and reported. Critics point out that the current methods do not provide meaningful feedback about student performance. For example, at the secondary level, the majority of American school districts rely on the Carnegie unit, which is based on a specified number of clock hours. In other words, students receive credit for the amount of time they spend in specific classes. This system has one major advantage: it can easily be standardized across schools, districts, and states. However, it also has the negative effect of rewarding "seat time" rather than demonstrated competence. All too many educators can cite specific examples of students who received credit for a course primarily because they showed up every day, not because they acquired any new knowledge or skills. A number of advocates for assessment reform are calling for a modification of this certification procedure to emphasize the role of demonstrated proficiency judged against established performance standards (Wiggins 1991).

The problems inherent to the Carnegie unit are also found in classroom record keeping and reporting practices. At the classroom level,

grades are the most common means of reporting a student's performance. Course grades are generally calculated by averaging the results of various measures. Unfortunately, this approach can too often result in a distorted picture of a student's true proficiency, because specific strengths and weaknesses are masked by the process of averaging. One student with a grade of "C" might perform very differently from another student with a grade of "C." And the letter grade by itself fails to suggest ways for students to improve their performance. What does a "C" grade tell a teacher or, more important, a student about how that student can improve?

An alternative approach to classroom reporting documents students' grasp of specific knowledge and skills. Because such a system is grounded by specific performance criteria, reports are more informative and meaningful to students, teachers, parents, and the general school community. If we wish to improve learning, not simply measure it, then we must reconsider our record-keeping and reporting mechanisms.

In summary, then, a revolution in assessment is necessary given (1) the changing nature of educational goals to encompass a broad array of academic and nonacademic competencies, (2) the need for assessment practices to enhance the learning and teaching processes, and (3) the need for record-keeping and reporting systems to provide accurate and useful information concerning students' mastery of specific knowledge and skills. Indeed, such a revolution is currently under way in the form of an emphasis on performance assessment.

What Is Performance Assessment?

This book is about performance assessment from the perspective of a specific model of teaching and learning, Dimensions of Learning. Although there is growing agreement on the need to reform assessment practices, no such consensus exists regarding assessment terminology. The terms *alternative assessment, authentic assessment,* and *performance assessment* are all used in discussions of assessment reform. Although these terms are sometimes used synonymously, they have different meanings. The term *alternative assessment* applies to any and all assessments that differ from the multiple-choice, timed, one-shot approaches that characterize most standardized and many classroom assessments. The term *authentic assessment,* popularized by Grant Wiggins (1989), conveys the idea that assessments should engage students in applying knowledge and skills in the same way they are used in the "real world" outside of school. Authentic assessment also reflects good instructional practice, so that teaching to the test is desirable. *Performance assessment* is a broad term, encompassing many of the characteristics of both authentic assessment and alternative assessment (Mitchell 1992).

In this book, performance assessment refers to variety of tasks and situations in which students are given opportunities to *demonstrate* their understanding and to thoughtfully *apply* knowledge, skills, and habits of mind in a variety of contexts. These assessments often occur over time and result in a tangible product or observable performance. They encourage self-evaluation and revision, require judgment to score, reveal degrees of proficiency based on established criteria, and make public the scoring criteria. They sometimes involve students working with others. In Chapter 3, we describe our model of performance assessment in detail. It is important to note from the outset, however, that an emphasis on performance assessment does not imply that we should abandon conventional testing. Instead, it reflects the belief that certain educational outcomes cannot be adequately assessed through conventional formats. Indeed, the current emphasis in performance assessment supports the practices that good teachers have always used to assess and improve learning: an array of data-gathering methods, including objective tests, observations, products, performances, and collections of student work.

The Role of Standards

Readers familiar with the current national discussion of standards-based education have no doubt noticed that our discussion of assessment reform has been laced with references to standards. Standards-based education is a rapidly growing movement within the larger movement of educational reform. It is intimately tied to performance assessment. In brief, standards-based education calls for a clearer identification of what students should know and be able to do. The emphasis on clearer educational goals stems from the research finding that what students are taught in a specific subject and at a specific grade level varies greatly among schools, and even among classrooms within a school. Indeed, this was the basic finding of many of the school effectiveness studies of the 1970s. For example, Fisher and his colleagues (1978) reported that one elementary school teacher who was observed for more than ninety days taught nothing about fractions, despite the state mandate to teach the topic at that grade level. When asked about the omission of this topic, the teacher responded, "I don't like fractions." Similarly, Berliner (1979) reported a range of over 4,000 minutes (a low of 5,749 minutes and a high of 9,965 minutes) in the time spent on reading instruction in four 4th grade classes. Again, teacher preference was the basic reason behind the variation.

The standards-based education movement grows out of the assumption that the only way to ensure that all students acquire specific knowledge and skills is to identify and teach to expected levels of performance for specific knowledge and skills. Schools and districts that have embraced the standards-based movement have made a concerted effort to identify critical knowledge and skills. These efforts, however, have disclosed a number of basic issues that must be confronted by anyone engaged in standards-based education. We will briefly consider three of these issues. (For a detailed discussion of the issues regarding standards-based education, see Marzano and Kendall 1993.)

Curriculum Standards Versus Content Standards

Clarifying the distinction between curriculum standards and content standards is a basic issue in standards-based education. Curriculum standards, sometimes referred to as program standards, are best described as the goals of classroom instruction. Content standards, also known as discipline standards, comprise the knowledge and skills specific to a given discipline.

Here are two standards from *Curriculum and Evaluation Standards* by the National Council of Teachers of Mathematics (1989):

a) develop spatial sense

b) describe, model, draw and classify shapes

The first standard describes a skill or ability a person might use in completing everyday tasks or academic problems. While driving a car, for instance, a person might use spatial sense to judge the distance of an upcoming turn. In mathematics class, a student might use spatial sense to solve a perplexing problem. The second standard is of a different sort because one does not usually model, draw, and classify shapes to complete everyday tasks or solve academic problems. Such activities are used more as instructional devices to help students understand shapes or demonstrate their understanding of shapes.

Standards like the first one above are called content standards because they describe information or skills essential to the practice or application of a particular discipline or content domain. Standards like the second one above are called curriculum standards because they identify the curricular or instructional activities that might be used to help students develop skill and ability within a given content domain. To a great extent, curriculum standards describe the instructional means to achieve content standards.

Knowledge and Skills Versus Performance

Some theorists describe standards in terms of knowledge and skills; others describe standards in terms of performance on specific tasks. For example, Albert Shanker, president of the American Federation of Teachers, defines a standard as "what we want youngsters to know and be able to do as a result of their education" (Shanker 1992, p. S11). For Shanker, identifying a standard involves identifying specific information or skills that must be mastered to gain expertise in a given domain. Diane Ravitch (1992), a former Assistant Secretary of Education, also describes standards from an information and skill perspective. Grant Wiggins, on the other hand, defines standards more in performance terms. For Wiggins (1989), a standard is a real-world, highly robust task that will, ideally, elicit or require the use of important knowledge and skills in various content domains. The emphasis on performance as the critical feature of a standard is also shared by the psychologists Shavelson, Baxter, and Pine (1992, p. 22), who state that standards should be "based on students' performance of concrete, meaningful tasks."

Content Standards Versus Lifelong Learning Standards

Content standards are those that refer to knowledge and skills belonging to a particular discipline. For example, a standard such as "understands and applies basic principles of number sense" is a content standard because it applies only to mathematics. A standard such as "makes and carries out effective plans," however, is not specific to any content area. In fact, it is not even specific to academics; it is a skill that can be used in virtually all aspects of life. This kind of standard is a lifelong learning standard because it is specific to no one discipline and can be used in many situations throughout a person's lifetime.

Standards, Performance Assessment, and Dimensions of Learning

In this book, we have taken a fairly specific position on the issues discussed above. First, we use the term *standard* to refer to knowledge and skills as opposed to instructional activities that should occur in the classroom. Thus, curriculum standards are not included in our standards. For us, the instructional implications of the Dimensions of Learning model represent de facto curriculum standards.

Second, we do not include performance standards in our definition of a standard. In effect, what we call *performance tasks* are a form of performance standard. In our model, teachers assess students by asking them to complete performance tasks that require them to meet identified standards. Standards and performance tasks maintain a symbiotic relationship. They are two interdependent and necessary components of a comprehensive assessment system. Marc Tucker, Co-director of the New Standards

Project, describes the necessary integration of standards and performance tasks:

> You can't assess kids' performance unless you give them the tasks, and you can't assess their degree of achievement unless they actually perform the tasks.
>
> But first you must be clear about what you want kids to know and be able to do. Those standards become the target for creating the assessment (Tucker 1992, p. 3).

Finally, we separate standards into two broad categories, content standards and lifelong learning standards. Content standards deal with the academic knowledge and skills belonging to a specific discipline. Lifelong learning standards deal with knowledge and skills that cut across all disciplines and are applicable to life outside the classroom.

Identifying specific content and lifelong learning standards is an important part of the assessment revolution in American education; it is a task we will tackle in the remainder of this book. Remember, however, that this task goes hand in hand with planning and delivering instruction that takes into account the constructivist nature of learning, a task which the *Dimensions of Learning Teacher's Manual* was designed to help teachers accomplish.

2

Assessment Standards Linked to the Five Dimensions of Learning

In Chapter 1, we discuss how performance assessment is intimately tied to the articulation of content standards and lifelong learning standards. In this chapter, we describe those standards in some depth. It is important to emphasize that our description of these standards is meant to be compatible with the Dimensions of Learning framework. We could, no doubt, have chosen another way of putting these standards to work; indeed, we could have devised categories other than "content standards" and "lifelong learning standards." But we believe the Dimensions of Learning framework has much to offer and that assessment standards linked to the five dimensions of learning will strengthen the framework.

Content Standards

One of the dominant themes of the current calls for educational reform is better knowledge of content. For example, the third of the six goals identified in the America 2000 proposal is that students will master complex content in mathematics, science, English, history, and geography by the year 2000 (Bush 1991). Mastery of content is obviously not a new concept. The heritage philosophy of education has always recognized that one of the primary functions of schools is to ensure that students acquire important disciplinary information and skills—what we think of as an academic heritage in the form of content standards. But exactly what are content standards?

In Chapter 1, we describe content standards as statements of what students should know and be able to do within specific disciplines. This delineation of knowing and doing is not arbitrary, but is based on current research and theory on the nature of knowledge. Researchers have found that content knowledge, whether it be in mathematics, science, or any other subject, can be divided into two distinct types of knowledge: declarative knowledge and procedural knowledge (Paris and Lindauer 1982; Paris, Lipson, and Wixson 1983).

Content Standards for Declarative Knowledge

Declarative knowledge can be thought of as *information* and can be ordered somewhat hierarchically according to its generality. At the bottom of the hierarchy are facts about specific persons, places, things, and events; at the top are concepts and generalizations. For example, the statement "John Kennedy was assassinated on November 22, 1963" is a fact. The statement "People holding high political office put their lives in jeopardy" is a generalization. The phrase "political assassinations" is a concept.

Although facts are important, generalizations and concepts help students develop a broad knowledge base because they transfer more readily to different situations. For instance, both the generalization about people in high political office and the concept of political assassinations can be applied across countries, situations, and ages, whereas the fact of Kennedy's assassination is a specific event that does not directly transfer to other situations. This is not to say that facts are unimportant. On the contrary, to truly understand generalizations and concepts, we must be able to support them with exemplifying facts. For instance, to understand the generalization about people in high political office, we need some understanding of a number of facts, one of which is probably that of Kennedy's assassination. Content standards for declarative knowledge are best formed using generalizations and concepts, because the knowledge of specific facts naturally falls under various concepts and generalizations. One cannot meet the standard of a generalization or concept without knowing the facts that support it.

Some content standards, then, are statements of the important concepts and generalizations in given content areas. To illustrate, here are some examples of content standards for declarative knowledge in several subject areas:

• *Science:* Understands that the universe is large and ancient on a scale staggering to the human mind.

• *Mathematics:* Understands the importance of geometry in the modern world.

• *History:* Recognizes that events in the past can inform the present.

• *Geography:* Recognizes that regions can be defined in cultural, physical, or political terms.

• *English:* Recognizes the role literature plays in developing the principles governing the lives of people in a given society.

Content Standards for Procedural Knowledge

Procedural knowledge can be thought of as *strategies or skills.* Like declarative knowledge, it can be ordered hierarchically according to its generality. At the bottom of the hierarchy are algorithms, which are procedures with steps that must be executed in a set order. Algorithms are commonly called skills. The procedure for doing three-column addition, for example, is a skill.

At the other end of the hierarchy are strategies that apply to a variety of situations, such as the general strategy of analyzing a novel problem, relating it to problems you're familiar with, and identifying important differences. Just as generalizations have related facts, strategies have related skills. For instance, to use a particular mathematics problem-solving strategy, students may need to use the skill of long division.

Given their inclusive nature, important strategies rather than skills should be the focus of content standards for procedural knowledge. Here are some examples of standards for procedural knowledge in several subjects:

• *Science:* Effectively uses the scientific method to ask and answer questions about the world.

• *Mathematics:* Accurately and efficiently transforms quantities in one system to those in other systems.

• *History:* Uses the process of historical research to ask and answer questions about the past.

• *Geography:* Accurately interprets and summarizes information from various types of maps, charts, and graphs.

• *English:* Uses the process of critical analysis to make informed judgments about literature.

How Many Content Standards to Identify

Identifying an appropriate and workable number of standards is critical to the success of any standards-based approach to education. Identifying too many standards is a real danger. Some schools employing a mastery learning approach to instruction have identified thousands of content standards, producing a system that is virtually impossible to implement because there is simply not enough time in the school year to teach and assess thousands of standards. Schools with too many content standards usually have expressed their standards in terms of facts and skills as opposed to concepts, generalizations, and strategies.

Schools that want to develop assessment standards don't have to start from scratch. Many recent national education reports provide useful guidance in identifying declarative and procedural standards. Although the reports present fairly exhaustive lists of the declarative and procedural knowledge that constitute competence in a given content area, they also identify the high-level generalizations and strategies, which are fairly limited in number. For example, the Bradley Report lists about 300 separate statements of knowledge and skill that are important to history, but only 12 of these are concepts, generalizations, or strategies (Bradley Commission on History in Schools 1991):

Highest Level Declarative Knowledge

- the past affects our private lives and society in general
- cultures are diverse yet share the human condition
- historical events happen in patterned ways
- while human intentions influence events, contextual factors interact with those events
- change and stability are equally as probable and natural
- not all problems have solutions
- because of personal characteristics specific individuals have made a difference in history both positively and negatively
- the nonrational, irrational and accidental alter history

- geography and history exist in a matrix or context of time and place

Highest Level Procedural Knowledge

- makes discerning judgments in public and personal life
- imposes a "present mind" perspective on past events
- avoids seizing upon particular lessons of history as cures for present ills

With minor wording changes, these statements easily become content standards. For instance, the leading statements in each category translate into the following standards:

- Understands and recognizes that the past affects our private lives.
- Effectively makes discerning judgments in public and personal life.

The Bradley Report, then, contains a relatively small number of high-level declarative and procedural standards that define what constitutes competence in history. Other national reports have similar distributions. For example, *Science for All Americans* (AAAS 1992) lists more than 2,000 pieces of declarative and procedural knowledge; only about 30, however, are concepts, generalizations, or strategies. In fact, all the traditional subject areas have a relatively small number of important concepts, generalizations, and strategies. Consequently, a school or district that wants to implement a manageable performance assessment system can begin by identifying the most important concepts, generalizations, and strategies in each subject area.

Lifelong Learning Standards

We have identified five categories of lifelong learning standards we consider particularly relevant to performance-based assessment and particularly compatible with the Dimensions of Learning framework:

1. Complex thinking standards
2. Information processing standards

3. Effective communication standards
4. Cooperation/collaboration standards
5. Effective habits of mind standards

We consider each in some depth.

Category 1: Complex Thinking Standards

This category contains two standards:

• Effectively uses a variety of complex reasoning strategies.

• Effectively translates issues and situations into manageable tasks that have a clear purpose.

In recent years, there has been intense interest in enhancing the complex reasoning abilities of students, primarily because national reports have shown that American students do not perform well on tasks that require complex reasoning. For example, reports from the National Assessment of Educational Progress (NAEP) have warned that students do poorly on tasks that involve "higher order thinking" (Burns 1986). A summary report from NAEP of twenty years of testing included this comment about American students' lack of ability to engage in complex reasoning:

> On an analytic task that asked students to compare food on the frontier (based on information presented) and today's food (based on their own knowledge), just 16 percent of the students at grade 8 and 27 percent at grade 12 provided an adequate or better response (Mullis, Owen, and Phillips 1990, p. 16).

Such poor performance by American students has even pushed the calls for strengthening students' reasoning skills to congressional hearings (Resnick 1987).

There have been many attempts to identify the various complex reasoning processes humans engage in. Although different researchers have given these processes a variety of names, they have generally recognized in them the same cognitive components. Here are thirteen of the most commonly identified processes:

- Comparing
- Classifying
- Induction
- Deduction
- Error Analysis
- Constructing Support
- Abstracting
- Analyzing Perspectives
- Decision Making
- Investigation
- Experimental Inquiry
- Problem Solving
- Invention

You can see the use of the first reasoning process, *comparing,* in the analytic task described in the NAEP excerpt above.

Dimensions of Learning includes all thirteen of these reasoning processes (they make up Dimensions 3 and 4). It is important to recognize that this list does not represent a hierarchy, a taxonomy, or even a list of discrete skills. It simply represents common types of tasks in which complex reasoning is exhibited.

The first of the two standards in the complex thinking category, "effectively uses of a variety of complex reasoning strategies," basically requires students to demonstrate their ability to competently use the thirteen reasoning processes listed above. If students can successfully complete tasks involving problem solving, invention, and so on, then they meet the standard of effectively using a variety of complex reasoning processes.

The second standard in this category, "effectively translates issues and situations into manageable tasks that have a clear purpose," is strongly linked to the first standard. Specifically, the thirteen reasoning processes listed above all represent specific ways of approaching issues and situations. In effect, the reasoning processes are ways of answering questions related to Dimensions 3 and 4. Figure 2.1 on page 20 contains examples of such questions

Students can demonstrate that they have met the standard of effectively translating issues and situations into manageable tasks that have a clear purpose by translating specific issues and situations into questions like those in Figure 2.1 and then answering those questions. For instance, a student might choose to translate the issues surrounding an upcoming presidential

FIGURE 2.1
Questions Related to
the Reasoning Processes of Dimensions 3 and 4

Questions	Reasoning Process	Dimension
How are these alike? How are they different?	Comparing	3
What groups can I put things into? What are the rules governing membership in these groups?	Classifying	3
What conclusions/generalizations can you draw from this, and what support do you have for these conclusions? What is the probability of this happening, and what support do you have for this conclusion?	Induction	3
What has to be true given the validity of this principle? What is the proof that this must be true?	Deduction	3
What's wrong with this? What specific errors have been made? How can it be fixed?	Error Analysis	3
What is the support for this argument? What are the limitations of this argument?	Constructing Support	3
What's the general pattern of information here? Where else does this apply? How can the information be represented in another way (graphically, symbolically)?	Abstracting	3
What do you think about this issue? On what do you base your opinion? What is another way of looking at the issue?	Analyzing Perspectives	3
What/whom would be the best or worst? Which one has the most or least?	decision making	4
What are the defining characteristics? Why/how did this happen? What would have happened if . . . ?	Definitional, Historical, and Projective Investigation	4
How can I overcome this obstacle? Given these conditions, what should I do to accomplish the goal?	Problem Solving	4
What do I observe? How can I explain it? What can I predict from it?	Experimental Inquiry	4
How can this be improved? What new thing is needed here?	Invention	4

election into a comparison task in which he identifies the similarities and differences between the candidates' positions. Another student might translate issues in that same situation into an error analysis task in which she analyzes the logical errors made by one or both candidates. In Chapter 3, we describe a specific technique for helping students meet this standard.

Category 2: Information Processing Standards

This category contains four standards:

•Effectively uses a variety of information-gathering techniques and information resources.

•Effectively interprets and synthesizes information.

•Accurately assesses the value of information.

•Recognizes where and how projects would benefit from additional information.

Complex tasks usually involve gathering and processing information from a variety of sources. In schools, reading and listening are by far students' primary information-gathering techniques; however, the information-rich world in which today's students will one day make their living calls for the use of additional techniques, such as interviewing and direct observation. To succeed, students will also need to be able to effectively use a variety of reference materials, primary sources, computerized data banks, and the like. One important standard in this category, then, is the ability to effectively use a variety of information-gathering techniques and information resources.

Another important standard concerns the ability to interpret and synthesize information. Regardless of how students gather information or where they find it, they must be able to effectively interpret and synthesize it if they are to really learn something. Interpretation and synthesis involve not just explicit information, but implicit information. This is because all information meant to be conveyed in a book, a film, or

even an interview is not explicit. Consequently, the effective information processor must consider that information which is not stated as well as that which is. Both types of information are then used to create a parsimonious synthesis of the information. One example of a task that tests students' ability to meet this standard is asking them to identify the main theme, main idea, and supporting details of an essay.

People usually gather information to help accomplish a specific task; often, however, not all of the information they've gathered is useful for accomplishing the task. In addition to accurately interpreting and synthesizing information, then, learners must be able to accurately determine whether the information gathered is relevant and valuable to the task at hand. This decision requires a keen understanding of both the nature of the task and the nature of the information. To be effective information processors, learners must meet the standard of accurately assessing the value of specific information to the completion of a given task.

Finally, effective information processors must meet the standard of recognizing how a project can benefit from additional information. They must be able to determine whether their information base is adequate to the task. And when they determine that their information base is inadequate, they need to seek new information. To demonstrate their ability to meet this standard, students generally must have the opportunity to work on projects over long periods of time, so they can continuously evaluate whether they need more information to satisfactorily complete a particular segment of the project.

Category 3: Effective Communication Standards

After completing a task, learners usually must communicate to others what they have learned, often by creating related products. In fact, almost all of us are at one time or another involved in communicating what we have learned, both at work and in our private lives.

We have developed five standards concerning effective communication and production:

- Expresses ideas clearly.
- Effectively communicates with diverse audiences.
- Effectively communicates in a variety of ways.
- Effectively communicates for a variety of purposes.
- Creates quality products.

When the product of a learning experience is a conclusion to be articulated, students must quite obviously express their ideas clearly. Whether the communication is a written essay, an oral report, an audiotaped report, or the like, ideas must be presented with a clear main point or theme and the appropriate supporting detail. Effective communicators meet the standard of expressing ideas clearly.

Another aspect of effective communication is the ability to communicate with diverse audiences. In school, those audiences should include peers, parents, experts, novices, the general public, and school board members. As students mature, they increase the types of audiences with which they can effectively communicate: while a primary student might be able to communicate with parents and teachers only, a high school student should be able to communicate with a wide span of audiences. According to current theory in rhetoric (Durst and Newell 1989), effectively communicating with any given audience demands a sensitivity to the level of knowledge of that audience and the interests of its members. Not considering these important aspects results in a communication that, although logically cohesive, probably won't be easily interpreted or enjoyed by the audience. Effective communicators meet the standard of communicating with a variety of audiences.

Skilled communicators also meet the standard of communicating in a variety of ways. Most schools emphasize two basic forms of communication, writing and speaking. In an information society, however, many other forms of communication are useful and appropriate:

- oral reports
- videotapes
- written reports
- panel discussions
- dramatic enactments
- outlines
- debates
- graphic representations
- newscasts
- discussions
- audiotapes
- flowcharts
- slide shows

All of these are effective tools for communicating information. Sometimes, however, learners may want to communicate emotion in addition to or in lieu of information, and choose to use other methods of communication:

- collages
- dances
- plays
- songs
- paintings
- pictures
- sculptures

Meeting the standard of communicating in a variety of ways, then, includes a facility with a variety of forms of communication.

Effective communicators must also be able to communicate for a variety of purposes—for instance, to inform, to persuade, to generate questions, or to elicit sympathy, anger, humor, pride, or joy. Researchers have shown that people who have the ability to write for specific purposes have some knowledge of specific rhetorical conventions (Durst and Newell 1989). Effective communicators understand and apply such conventions.

Finally, effective communicators meet the standard of creating quality products. They know the accepted criteria for the product they are creating and make sure the product meets or exceeds those criteria.

Category 4: Collaboration/Cooperation Standards

One of the major educational realizations of the past decade is that adults often work in groups, rather than independently, to complete tasks. Although the importance of cooperation and collaboration has been recognized in the workplace for decades, educators have only recently given it their attention, primarily as a result of the work of Roger and David Johnson (1987) and Robert Slavin (1983).

We have developed four standards concerning effective collaboration and cooperation:

• Works toward the achievement of group goals.
   • Effectively uses interpersonal skills.
   • Contributes to group maintenance.
   • Effectively performs a variety of roles.

While a person might be quite skilled at working toward an individual goal, she might not be skilled at working toward a group goal. This latter ability requires a person to make a commitment to the group goal and effectively carry out assigned roles. Learners who are skilled at collaboration and cooperation can meet the standard of working toward the achievement of group goals.

Effective performance within a group also involves the use of interpersonal skills, such as participating in group interactions with little or no prompting and expressing ideas and opinions in a manner sensitive to the feelings and knowledge base of others. The learner skilled at collaboration and cooperation knows how to empower his fellow group members through interpersonal skills.

The standard of contributing to group maintenance involves identifying changes or modifications necessary in the group process and then working to carry out those changes. Just as an individual must know when he should change his plan of attack, so too must a group. The individual skilled at collaboration and cooperation contributes to keeping the group on track.

Finally, effective collaboration and cooperation means meeting the standard of effectively performing a variety of roles in a group. Within a well-functioning group, members play a variety of roles. Some members are information gatherers, others are facilitators. Still others continually keep track of resources and progress toward the goals, and so on. The individual skilled at working within a group can perform a variety of roles.

Category 5: Habits of Mind Standards

Researchers in the field of cognitive psychology have found that human beings, unlike any other animal, have the ability to control their own behavior, even their own thought processes, by using effective habits of mind. Ennis (1987), Paul (1990), Costa (1991), Perkins (1984), Flavell (1976), Zimmerman (1990) and Amabile (1983) place the effective habits of mind in three broad categories: self-regulation, critical thinking, and creative thinking. We have identified standards for each of these three areas:

Self-Regulation
   a. Is aware of own thinking.
   b. Makes effective plans.
   c. Is aware of and uses necessary resources.
   d. Is sensitive to feedback.
   e. Evaluates the effectiveness of own actions.

Critical Thinking
   f. Is accurate and seeks accuracy.
   g. Is clear and seeks clarity.
   h. Is open-minded.
   i. Restrains impulsivity.
   j. Takes a position when the situation warrants it.
   k. Is sensitive to the feelings and level of knowledge of others.

Creative Thinking
   l. Engages intensely in tasks even when answers or solutions are not immediately apparent.

m. Pushes the limits of own knowledge and abilities.

n. Generates, trusts, and maintains own standards of evaluation.

o. Generates new ways of viewing a situation outside the boundaries of standard conventions.

The general category of habits of mind also constitutes Dimension 5 of the Dimensions of Learning model. This category contains the most standards, underscoring the importance of the habits of mind, which directly affect the other standards. For example, if a student is pushing the limits of his knowledge and ability, he will likely meet many of the other lifelong learning standards as well as the content standards.

The Standards and Dimensions of Learning

The content standards and five categories of lifelong learning standards are highly compatible with Dimensions of Learning. In fact, as mentioned earlier, some are taken directly from the Dimensions of Learning framework. Recall from Chapter 1 that the framework assumes that five aspects of thinking are basic to every effective learning situation:

• *Dimension 1:* Positive attitudes and perceptions about learning
• *Dimension 2:* Thinking needed to acquire and integrate new knowledge
• *Dimension 3:* Thinking needed to extend and refine knowledge
• *Dimension 4:* Thinking needed to use knowledge meaningfully
• *Dimension 5:* Use of effective habits of mind

The five dimensions of learning implicitly and explicitly address all six categories of standards. For instance, in providing direction for the acquisition and integration of knowledge, Dimension 2 refers to the attainment of content standards, thus explicitly addressing the content standards category. Dimensions 3 and 4 explicitly address the complex thinking category; in fact, the thirteen complex reasoning processes identified in this category are drawn directly from Dimensions 3 and 4. Likewise, the standards in the category of effective habits of mind are drawn directly from Dimension 5: they are the habits of mind identified in Dimensions of Learning.

In summary, content standards, complex thinking standards, and effective habits of mind standards are explicitly addressed in Dimensions 2, 3, 4, and 5. The other categories of standards— information processing, effective communication, and collaboration/cooperation—are addressed implicitly by Dimensions of Learning in the types of classroom tasks that teachers and students create using Dimensions of Learning.

Tasks based on the reasoning processes of Dimension 3 and 4 are perfect vehicles for incorporating standards from the categories not explicit in the model. To illustrate, consider the following Dimension 4 decision-making task that might be presented to students in a social studies class:

Remember that some people believe, perhaps despairingly, that there are only two things on which we can depend, death and taxes. Think about the kinds of taxes you have been studying— the method of collection, the amount of money that is generated, who pays them, the possible uses of the money, and the way people have historically reacted to them.

Pretend you are a legislator with the job of recommending a tax to fund the schools in your area. You are also up for reelection within six months. Select the kind of tax that you will recommend. Then, pretend you are a senior citizen with a fixed income and your children are grown and living in another state. You must, again, recommend a kind of tax to be levied in order to fund schools. For both situations, be ready to explain the kinds of taxes you considered, the criteria you used in making your selection, and your final decision.

The achievement of standards in the information processing category is a necessary part of tasks like this one. The Dimension 3 and 4 tasks require students to gather information in a variety of ways from a variety of sources, and so on. To accomplish this decision-making task, students might have to gather information from their textbook, from magazines, from newscasts, and the like. Tasks organized around the reasoning processes of Dimensions 3 and 4, then, quite naturally involve the standards from the information processing category.

Similarly, Dimension 3 and 4 tasks implicitly involve the standards from the effective communication category. As students engage in these tasks, they must communicate conclusions in various ways and create various products. In the decision-making task, for instance, students might be asked to write a report of their findings and produce a newscast, a videotape, or an audiotape. And they might be asked to communicate their conclusions to different audiences.

Finally, the Dimension 3 and 4 tasks are ideal vehicles for gathering information that shows whether students are meeting the standards of collaboration and cooperation. As students work on tasks in cooperative groups, they have the opportunity to exhibit their ability to meet standards like "works toward the achievement of group goals" and "demonstrates effective interpersonal skills."

The standards we describe here are similar to those identified by many schools and districts involved in restructuring. Thus, schools or districts that have already identified standards can use the ideas in this book to create a performance-based assessment system geared directly toward specific standards. And they can use the Dimensions of Learning instructional model to help teachers provide systematic instruction that enables students meet the standards. As mentioned previously, the *Dimensions of Learning Teacher's Manual* provides systematic guidance in how to use the Dimensions of Learning framework as an instructional system. In the remaining chapters of this book, we describe how to create a comprehensive performance assessment system that supports standards-based education.

3

How We Assess Performance

Performance Tasks

In Chapter 2, we saw that the Dimensions of Learning model explicitly and implicitly addresses both the content standards and lifelong learning standards of standards-based education. We also saw that performance tasks constructed around Dimensions 3 and 4 are important tools for assessing students' ability to meet standards. If you're familiar with Dimensions of Learning, you'll know that these tasks have two basic characteristics.

First, performance tasks require an extended period of time to complete. The vast majority of the tasks students are asked to perform in school are anything but long-term in nature. In fact, research suggests that most classroom tasks can be completed in a single thirty- to sixty-minute period (Doyle 1983, Fisher and Hiebert 1988). Research and theory also tell us, however, that the "deepest" types of learning occur when learners have the time to engage themselves in increasingly more sophisticated "layers" of investigation and explanation of content, with each layer bringing new insights and new learnings (Jaques 1985). Layered tasks, of course, cannot be completed in a single class period; in fact, students frequently work on layered tasks over a span of two, three, or even four weeks. Consequently, within our framework, one criterion for effective performance tasks is that they require students to work on them over an extended period of time.

Second, performance tasks require students to construct new knowledge. Most of the tasks students are now asked to complete have one predetermined "right" answer that is usually a single piece of information. Tasks requiring students to fill in the blanks, match answers, or select the correct response from among a list of alternatives (i.e., multiple-choice) all use a predetermined single-answer format. In these tasks, there is no room for diversity of response; a specific answer is clearly correct, others are clearly incorrect. Even most essay tasks have fairly specific answers, so writing a paragraph or two in response to a question does not always require students to construct new knowledge. Yet it is this very process of constructing knowledge that is essential to effective learning. For the most effective learning to occur, students must be allowed to articulate a unique position and defend it (Vosniadou and Brewer 1987). The second criterion for effective performance tasks, then, is that they require students to construct new knowledge.

How to Construct Performance Tasks

Performance tasks are presented to students as part of regular classroom instruction. The key to using the tasks to assess students' ability to meet identified standards lies in constructing the tasks to explicitly include selected standards. A number of models for generating performance tasks have been developed (see Archbald and Newmann 1988; Baker et al. 1992; Herman, Aschbacher, and Winters 1992; Katz and Chard 1990). The process we describe here is designed to be compatible with the Dimensions of Learning framework.

Step 1

Identify a content standard that will be included in the task. A basic premise underlying the construction of performance tasks is that they include important content standards. Recall from Chapter 2 that content standards are statements of high-level declarative and procedural knowledge. For example, a history teacher might decide to assess students' declarative knowledge by including this content standard in a performance task: "Understands that war forces sensitive issues to surface and causes people to confront inherent conflicts of values and beliefs." A mathematics teacher, on the other hand, might include in his task a standard for assessing procedural knowledge: "Effectively and accurately transforms quantities in one metric to those in another." As discussed in Chapter 2, it is important that the declarative or procedural information identified for a content standard be stated in very general terms. Ideally, a school or district will have identified content standards, so that individual teachers do not have to originate all of them.

Step 2

Structure the task around one of the complex reasoning in processes in Dimensions 3 and 4. The complex reasoning processes in Dimensions 3 and 4 are the heart of both the Dimensions of Learning model and the performance tasks. When first constructing a performance task, you may find it helpful to use one of these reasoning processes to frame the task. To illustrate, consider the history standard described in Step 1: "Understands that war forces

sensitive issues to surface and causes people to confront inherent conflicts of values and beliefs." When constructing a performance task for this standard, the history teacher considers a few possibilities based on several of the reasoning processes from Dimensions 3 and 4:

Comparison (Dimension 3):	Compare the public reaction during World War II to that during the Vietnam war.
Error Analysis (Dimension 3):	Identify the errors in reasoning made by those responsible for interring Japanese Americans during World War I.
Constructing Support (Dimension 3):	Refute or support the claim that the atomic bomb had to be dropped to end World War II.
Decision Making (Dimension 4):	What other alternatives could the United States have used to end the war?
Investigation (Dimension 4):	Why did Japan attack Pearl Harbor? Some say Roosevelt intentionally provoked the Japanese. Others disagree.
Problem Solving (Dimension 4):	If you were the President of the United States during World War II, how would you force the unconditional surrender of Japan without using the atomic bomb and yet provide for a secure postwar world.

Although all of these reasoning processes are solid building blocks for performance tasks, a few seem more strongly linked than others to the identified standard. The guiding principle when developing a performance task is to select the reasoning process that most strongly emphasizes the content information identified in Step 1. Given the standard identified here, the history teacher concludes that a decision-making task is most appropriate.

Step 3

Write a first draft of the performance task, incorporating the information identified in steps 1 and 2. Constructing an effective performance task is much like crafting a well-written composition. The author must take the description of the task through a number of drafts to achieve excellence. Hence, the task created at this step should be considered the first of many drafts. By combining the history standard identified in Step 1 with the reasoning process identified in Step 2, the history teacher constructs this performance task:

> President Harry S. Truman has requested that you serve on a White House task force. The goal is to decide how to force the unconditional surrender of Japan, yet provide for a secure postwar world.
>
> You are now a member of a committee of four and have reached the point at which you are trying to decide whether to drop the bomb. Identify the alternatives you are considering and the criteria you are using to make the decision. Explain the values that influenced the selection of the criteria and the weights you placed on each. Also explain how your decision has helped you better understand this statement: "War forces people to confront inherent conflicts of values."

Remember, creating an effective performance task is an iterative process. Few people are able to create a well-developed task on the first try.

Step 4

Identify standards from the information processing category to include in the task, and revise the task to make these standards explicit. Almost any performance task will require students to collect and process information, usually from multiple sources. Consequently, such tasks are perfect vehicles for gathering assessment information for the standards in the information processing category. To obtain information for a standard in this category, however, the task drafted in Step 3 must be revised to explicitly require students to demonstrate the ability to meet a given standard. Let's say the history teacher decides to gather information about students' ability to meet the standard "accurately assesses the value of information." She adds specific directions to the task relating to that standard:

> As you work on your task, try to use a variety of sources of information—books, magazine articles, newspapers, and people who lived through the war. Keep a list of those sources and be prepared to describe how you determined which information was most relevant and which information was not very useful.

Step 5

Identify standards (if any) from the habits of mind category and the collaboration/cooperation category to include in the task, and revise the task to make these standards explicit. If the history teacher wants to gather information regarding one or more of the standards in the habits of mind category, the collaboration/cooperation category, or both these categories, she again makes those standards explicit in the task. For example, she adds the following directions to the task so she can use it to obtain information regarding the standard "makes effective plans":

> Before you begin your task, establish a clear goal and write it down. Then write down a plan for accomplishing your goal. When you are finished with the task, be prepared to describe the changes you had to make in your plan along the way.

Likewise, if the teacher wants to gather assessment information for the collaborative/cooperative worker standard "contributes to group maintenance," she again adds explicit directions to the task:

> While working on your task, you will be collaborating in small groups with some of your classmates. As you work together, you will find that you must change certain things you are doing to make your group work more effectively. Be aware of your

behavior in the group. Keep track of those behaviors you had to change and what you did to change them.

Step 6

Identify specific standards from the effective communication category and build them into the task. Ultimately, every performance task results in some type of communication or product, the standards for which are part of the effective communication category. Again, to ensure that information is gathered on the selected standards in this category, the teacher revises the performance task to make the standards explicit. To illustrate, assume that the history teacher selects the standard "effectively communicates through a variety of mediums." She then adds explicit directions to the task to obtain information on the standard:

Present your conclusions and findings in at least two of the following ways:
- a written report
- a letter to the President following the completion of the committee meeting
- an article written for *Time* magazine, complete with suggested photos and charts
- a videotape of a dramatization of the committee meeting
- an audiotape
- a newscast
- a mock interview

Teachers can create performance tasks that will provide explicit information about students' ability to achieve selected content standards and lifelong learning standards. Proficiencies from no more than three or four of the categories of standards should ever be included on any one task, because a manageable task including content standards and standards from all five lifelong learning categories is very complex and difficult to design. Chapter 5 contains examples of performance tasks that address specific content and lifelong learning standards.

Rubrics for Scoring Performance Tasks

As with most real-world tasks, performance tasks do not have a single correct answer; there are a variety of ways to successfully complete them. Consequently, students' performance of the tasks cannot be "machine scored," but must be judged by one or more persons guided by well-defined criteria. This approach is similar to that used for judging performances in gymnastics or diving competitions.

The vehicle used to guide human judgment is a rubric, which has its origins in the Latin *rubrica terra*, referring to the use of red earth centuries ago to mark or signify something of importance. Today we maintain the spirit of this original meaning, since the term commonly means an authoritative or established rule. More specifically, a scoring rubric consists of a fixed scale and a list of characteristics describing performance for each of the points on the scale. Because rubrics describe levels of performance, they provide important information to teachers, parents, and others interested in what students know and can do. Rubrics also *promote* learning by offering clear performance targets to students for agreed-upon standards.

Rubrics are presented to students along with the performance task. If a task is designed to measure three standards, the teacher produces three sets of rubrics. Developing rubrics can be quite time-consuming, so we have streamlined the process for you by including in this book rubrics for content standards and for the standards in the five lifelong learning categories. These rubrics appear in Chapter 6. Think of them as blueprints for writing more specific rubrics. As you construct your own performance tasks, you can adapt one of the basic rubrics to assess students' achievement of the specific standards included in the task, particularly the content standards. There are two generic rubrics for content standards, one for declarative standards and one for procedural standards. We'll use the generic rubric for declarative content standards, reproduced below, to illustrate how to adapt the rubrics to specific content:

4 Demonstrates a thorough understanding of the generalizations, concepts, and facts specific to the task or situation. Provides new insights into some aspect of that information.

3 Displays a complete and accurate understanding of the generalizations, concepts, and facts specific to the task or situation.

2 Displays an incomplete understanding of the generalizations, concepts, and facts specific to the task or situation and has some notable misconceptions.

1 Demonstrates severe misconceptions about the generalizations, concepts, and facts specific to the task or situation.

This scale runs from 1 to 4, with 4 describing the highest level of performance and 1 describing the lowest level of performance. Usually one level of a rubric is considered the accepted level of performance. In the four-point rubrics provided in this book, 3 is the accepted level of performance. Thus, for the rubric above, the accepted level of performance is that students display a complete and accurate understanding of the generalizations, concepts, and facts built into the performance task.

In the history example we've been looking at in this chapter, the generalization built into the task is that "war forces sensitive issues to surface and causes people to confront inherent conflicts of values." The teacher who created the performance task adapts the generic rubric so that it specifies the generalization built into the task:

4 Demonstrates a thorough understanding of the generalization that war forces sensitive issues to surface and causes people to confront inherent conflicts of values. Provides new insights into people's behavior during wartime.

3 Displays a complete and accurate understanding of the generalization that war forces sensitive issues to surface and causes people to confront inherent conflicts of values.

2 Displays an incomplete understanding of the generalization that war forces sensitive issues to surface and causes people to confront inherent conflicts of values and has some notable misconceptions about this generalization.

1 Demonstrates severe misconceptions about the generalization that war forces sensitive issues to surface and causes people to confront inherent conflicts of values.

The teacher then adapts rubrics for the other standards measured by the task. That is, she adapts the generic rubrics in Chapter 6 so that they address the specific standards built into the performance task. Once the teacher has prepared the rubrics, she presents them to students so they are aware of the standards on which they will be assessed and the levels of performance expected by the teacher.

Upon completion of the performance task, the teacher uses the rubrics to score students on the standards she built into the task. A Task Evaluation Form like the one in Figure 3.1 helps the teacher efficiently record scores. Figure 3.1 shows that Bill Johnson has received a score of 3 on the standard "understands that war forces sensitive issues to surface and causes people to confront inherent conflicts of values," a 2 on the standard "accurately assesses the value of information," and a 4 on the standard "effectively communicates in a variety of ways." The teacher assigned these scores using the three rubrics written to assess the three standards built into the task. Chapter 9 contains a blank Task Evaluation Form that you may photocopy for your own use.

Performance tasks are the backbone of a performance assessment system. They can be constructed to provide assessment information for any and all content and lifelong learning standards.

FIGURE 3.1
Task Evaluation Form

Student ___Bill Johnson___

STANDARDS	EVALUATION			
Understands that war forces sensitive issues and forces people to confront values	1	2	③	4
Accurately assesses the value of information	1	②	3	4
Effectively communicates in a variety of ways	1	2	3	④
	1	2	3	4
	1	2	3	4
	1	2	3	4
	1	2	3	4
	1	2	3	4
	1	2	3	4

Student-Constructed Performance Tasks

In the previous section, we described how a teacher can design a performance task to assess specific content and lifelong learning standards. Sometimes, however—and more frequently, we hope—students should be encouraged to create their own performance tasks. Joan Baron, a noted expert on performance assessment, explains that for a performance task to be "authentic" it must include five characteristics, one of which is that it be constructed or framed by students. Baron's (1991) five criteria for authentic assessment are:

1. The task is meaningful both to teachers and students.

2. The task is framed by the student.

3. The task requires the student to locate and analyze information as well as draw conclusions about it.

4. The task requires students to communicate results clearly.

5. The task requires students to work together for at least part of the task.

Students obviously cannot construct tasks in the same way a teacher does. We recommend that teachers use the five-step process outlined here to help students construct their own performance tasks.

Step 1

Have students identify a question related to something in the current unit of study that interests them. When students construct their own performance tasks, they usually do so by identifying a question that interests them. We suggest that teachers ask students to use the questions that correspond to the thinking processes from Dimensions 3 and 4 to help them shape their questions (see Figure 2.1 on page 20). These questions can easily be rewritten to guide students in this first step of constructing their own performance tasks, as shown in Figure 3.2.

To illustrate how these questions might be used, assume that a student is studying about John F. Kennedy. When asked to create a performance task, the student begins by identifying a question similar to one of the questions in Figure 3.2 that he wants to answer as a result of studying Kennedy. After examining the list, the student identifies the question "What would have happened if John F. Kennedy had not been assassinated?" In effect, the student has identified a possible event he wants to explore. This question is the foundation of the student's performance task.

Step 2

Help students write a first draft of the task that makes explicit one or more of the reasoning processes from Dimensions 3 and 4. Using the basic question identified by the student, the teacher helps the student write a first draft of the performance task. The process of drafting the task will itself provide valuable information about a student's ability to effectively translate issues and situations into meaningful tasks that have a clear purpose. Recall from Chapter 2 that this is one of the standards in the complex thinking category (see page 19). Having students create their own performance tasks is one of the best ways to gather assessment information for this standard.

Helping a student identify the reasoning process on which the performance task is based is an important part of the process of drafting the task, because the reasoning process provides focus for the task and direction for the student. The question raised by the student interested in John F. Kennedy applies to projective investigation. Examining page 169 of the *Dimensions of Learning Teacher's Manual,* we find that projective investigation involves the following process:

1. Clearly identifying the hypothetical event.
2. Identifying what is already known or agreed upon about the hypothetical event.
3. Identifying and explaining the contradictions and confusions about the hypothetical event.
4. Developing and defending a plausible resolution to the confusion or contradiction.

Using this process as a guide, the student writes a first draft of his task:

> I'm going to examine what might have happened if John F. Kennedy had not been assassinated. I will identify what other people have written about this possibility and then take and defend my own position.

Step 3

Help students identify standards from the categories of: (1) information processing, (2) effective communication, (3) habits of mind, and (4) collaboration/ cooperation. The student now considers other lifelong learning standards he might want to incorporate into his performance task. Here it is important to recall Baron's list of the criteria for an authentic task (see page 31). Following Baron's suggestions, students should be encouraged to select standards from the information processing category, the effective communication category, and the collaboration/cooperation category. In this instance, the student decides that he wants to incorporate the following standards into his performance task:

FIGURE 3.2
Stimulus Questions Derived from
the Reasoning Processes of Dimensions 3 and 4

Stimulus Question	Reasoning Process	Dimension
Do you want to determine how certain things are similar and different?	Comparing	3
Do you want to organize things into groups? Do you want to identify the rules or characteristics that have been used to form groups?	Classifying	3
Are there specific pieces of information that you want to draw conclusions about?	Induction	3
Are there specific rules you see operating here? Are there things that you know must happen?	Deduction	3
Are there errors in reasoning you want to describe? Are there errors being performed in a process?	Error Analysis	3
Is there a position you want to defend on a particular issue?	Constructing Support	3
Do you see a relationship that no one else has seen? What is the abstract pattern or theme that is at the heart of the relationship?	Abstracting	3
Are there differing perspectives on an issue you want to explore?	Analyzing Perspectives	3
Is there an important decision that should be studied or made?	Decision Making	4
Is there some new idea or new theory that should be described in detail?	Definitional Investigation	4
Is there something that happened in the past that should be studied?	Historical Investigation	4
Is there a possible or hypothetical event that should be studied?	Projective Investigation	4
Do you want to describe how some obstacle can be overcome?	Problem Solving	4
Is there a prediction you want to make and then test?	Experimental Inquiry	4
Is there something you want to improve upon? Is there something new you want to create?	Invention	4

- Accurately assesses the value of information (from the information processing category).
- Expresses ideas clearly (from the effective communication category).
- Assesses and monitors one's own performance in a group (from the collaboration/cooperation category).

Step 4

Help students rewrite the task so that it highlights the standards identified in Step 3. Once the student has identified new standards, he rewrites the task to make the standards explicit. The student in our example rewrites his task in the following way:

> I'm going to examine what might have happened if John F. Kennedy had not been assassinated. I will identify what other people have written on this topic. Working with two other people who have identified similar topics, I will gather information from various sources. While working with my research partners, I will keep track of how well I monitor my behavior in the group. As I collect my research information, I will keep track of the most relevant information and the information that is interesting but not as relevant and report on this. After I have collected enough information, I will take a position and defend it, taking special care to express my ideas clearly.

Step 5

Help students write the rubrics for the standards that have been built into the task. With the task fully designed, the teacher helps the student write rubrics that will be used to assess the student's performance on the standards. Again, the rubrics in Chapter 6 can serve as blueprints. The student selects rubrics for those standards that have been built into the task. A useful convention in this step of the

process is for the student to write the rubrics in the first person. Here is an example of how a student might rewrite the appropriate generic rubric in Chapter 6 for the standard "expresses ideas clearly":

4   I have communicated my position clearly. In addition, I have provided support that is very detailed and very rich.

3   I have presented my position clearly. I have provided adequate support and detail.

2   I have presented some important information, but I have no clear position.

1   I have communicated only isolated pieces of information.

To help you aid students in the process of writing rubrics, we have included student versions of the various rubrics in Chapter 8.

After writing the rubrics, the student completes the task. Then he uses his rubrics to score his performance on the standards that have been built into the task. The student may do this with the aid of the teacher, or the teacher and student may independently calculate their scores and then compare them.

If you compare this process with the earlier process for teacher-designed performance tasks, you will note one major difference: that teacher-designed tasks begin with content standards, whereas student-designed tasks make no mention of them. When students are designing their own tasks, they should be allowed to do so without any constraints on the declarative or procedural content knowledge addressed in the task. Teacher-designed performance tasks, on the other hand, are excellent vehicles for addressing specific content standards in a performance format. Whether they are designed by teachers or students, performance tasks are powerful tools for learning and assessment and should be used frequently.

Other Ways of Gathering Assessment Information

Performance tasks are not the only way to gather information about students' ability to achieve content standards and lifelong learning standards. At least three other means provide useful information: student self-assessment, naturalistic observation, and traditional teacher-made tests.

Student Self-Assessment

Within the last decade, student self-assessment has received serious consideration as a valid means of assessment. For example, Tierney, Carter, and Desai (1991) assert that student self-assessment is at the heart of the performance assessment movement. There is no reason why students cannot assess themselves on all content and lifelong learning standards. For example, while studying a complex concept such as "meiosis" in science, students might be asked to rate their understanding of that concept. Similarly, while solving a problem, students might be asked to assess the extent to which they are meeting one or more of the habits of mind standards.

Although the rubrics we described earlier can help students conduct self-assessment in the context of a performance task, there are other ways of collecting student self-assessment data. Perhaps the most powerful tool a student can use is a journal. Student journals have been used extensively in literacy development (Atwell 1987, Calkins 1986, Macrorie 1984). When accompanied by the use of probes, however, they become an excellent aid to student self-assessment. A probe is nothing more than a question asked by the teacher to elicit assessment information for specific standards. Figure 3.3 shows a few examples of probes for the various types of standards.

Students write their responses to probes like these in their journals, and the teacher periodically collects the journals to review each student's responses. The teacher meets individually

---

FIGURE 3.3

Examples of Probes

- **Probe for a Content Standard:** "Describe the extent to which you understand the information about tornadoes that we have covered. What are you confused about? What are you confident about?"

- **Probe for a Complex Thinking Standard:** "Describe how effective you have been so far in your investigation task."

- **Probe for an Information Processing Standard:** "Describe how effective you have been in gathering information for your project."

- **Probe for a Communication Standard:** "Describe how effective you have been in communicating your conclusions."

- **Probe for a Habits of Mind Standard:** "Describe how well you have used the competencies of seeking accuracy throughout your project."

- **Probe for a Collaboration/Cooperation Standard:** "Describe how well you have worked with your group throughout your project."

with students to discuss the responses. Thus, student responses as well as student/teacher conferences about those responses become assessment data for the content and lifelong learning standards.

Naturalistic Observation ("Kid Watching")

As the name implies, naturalistic observation or "kid watching" occurs as teachers and students go about their daily work. When kid watching, teachers simply look for and record behaviors that provide evidence of students' competence in the various standards. For example, while students work on cooperative projects, teachers pay particular attention to students' interactions, recording specific behaviors or interpretations of specific behaviors that allow them to assess the collaboration/cooperation standards. Similarly, while students are engaged in various classroom activities, teachers note behaviors that indicate how well students are meeting the various standards from the habits of mind category.

Traditional Teacher-Made Tests

Some teachers incorrectly assume that the performance assessment movement implies an end to traditional forms of teacher-made tests, such as multiple-choice, short-answer, and true/false tests. These kinds of tests are still powerful assessment devices, particularly for content standards. In fact, multiple choice, true/false, matching, fill-in-the-blank, and essay tests can be effective tools for assessing students' understanding of declarative content, simply because they are highly focused and efficient.

*   *   *

In this chapter, we have presented basic processes for constructing teacher-made performance tasks and student-made performance tasks. We have also briefly discussed other methods of collecting assessment information. All of these means of assessment have an important role in a comprehensive performance assessment system.

4

Keeping Track of Performance

One of the most challenging aspects of developing a comprehensive performance assessment system is developing a way to keep records of student performance. In educators' eyes, record keeping is the bane of most performance assessment efforts. In this chapter, we discuss record keeping at the classroom level and at the school or district level.

Assessment in the Classroom

In a comprehensive performance assessment system, one of the teacher's jobs is to keep track of student performance on selected standards. We believe that no one teacher should be expected to assess students on all standards, but that different teachers should be responsible for different standards. For instance, let's say in a typical elementary school, a 5th grade teacher is responsible for assessing students' ability to meet six content standards, one complex reasoning standard, two information processing standards, one communication standard, one habits of mind standard, and two collaboration/cooperation standards. In all, the teacher is responsible for collecting assessment information on thirteen standards.

As described in the previous chapter, the teacher collects information on these thirteen standards using teacher-constructed and student-constructed performance tasks, naturalistic observation, student self-assessment, and traditional tests. The teacher records student performance using a Grade Book Form like the one shown in Figure 4.1. (Chapter 9 contains a blank Grade Book Form.) For each standard, the form provides space to record scores for specific tasks or situations.

Consider the column in Figure 4.1 marked "C". The "C" signifies that the information in that column is about a content standard, and the teacher writes the standard immediately below the "C" designation, in the row titled "Standards." In this example, the standard is "understands that key people have influenced history." In the next row, labeled "Assessment Key," the teacher notes the type of assessment used. In this example, the scores for specific tasks or situations came from a 15th century task (a performance task), two tests, and a research project.

Now consider the first student's scores on these assessments. The first student, Bill Johnson, received a score of 3 on the 15th century performance task (a task concerning information about the 15th century), a score of 3 on a research project, and scores of 2 and 3 (out of 4) on two tests. The teacher arrived at these scores using the rubrics for specific tasks and situations found in Chapter 6 and translating the classroom tests into a four-point scale.

Figure 4.1
Grade Book Form

STANDARD CATEGORY	C		HM		CT		EC		C	
STANDARD	-key people influence history -knowledge of 15th and 16th century		-seeks perspectives and considers choices		-uses a variety of complex reasoning		-communicates in a variety of ways		-regions can be defined culturally, politically, and physically	
ASSESSMENT KEY (top)	15th century task	2 tests	15th century task	Observ. 9/9 11/20	15th century task/ decision making	Third world task def investig.	Third world task (panel)	Essay assign.	Columbus task	Third world task
ASSESSMENT KEY (bottom)	Research project	Summary Validation		Summary Validation	Columbus task/ compare	Summary Validation	Oral present.	Summary Validation	Homework 10/1 12/3	Summary Validation
Student Names										
Bill Johnson	3	2, 3	4	4, 3	4	4	3	2	4	3
	3	3			4	4	3	3	3, 4	3
Jannie Pullock	4	4, 3	2	2, 2	3	3	3	2	4	4
	4	4			2	3	1		4, 4	4
Whisler, Jo Sue	2	4	3	3	4	4	3	3	2	3
	4	3			4	4	3	3	3	3
Kendall, John	2	1	3	2, 2	1	1	1		1	2
	–				1	1			1, 2	2
Paynter, Diane	2	3, 4	3	3	2	3	3	3	3	3
	2	2			2	2	4	4	3, 3	3
Mayeski, Fran	4	4, 4	3	3	3	1	3	3	4	4
	4	4					2	3	4, 4	4
Grady, Joan	3	3, 3	3	3	2	2	4	4	3	3
	2	3			3	2			3, 3	3

38

Summary Validations

The Grade Book Form also provides space for a summary score or "summary validation" for each student on each standard. As the name implies, a summary validation is the result of considering a student's performance across the various situations and tasks. To make this summary judgment, the teacher uses summary rubrics. Chapter 7 contains the summary rubrics for the content standards and lifelong learning standards. To illustrate how a teacher uses these rubrics, consider the summary rubric for the standard listed in the fourth large column of the grade book, "Communicates in a variety of ways." It is one of the standards in the effective communication category, as signified by "EC" at the top of the column. The summary rubric for this standard is:

4 Demonstrates an ability to communicate in a wide and diverse variety of ways.

3 Demonstrates an ability to communicate in different ways.

2 Demonstrates an ability to communicate in a restricted range of ways.

1 Does not demonstrate the ability to communicate in a variety of ways.

To obtain the summary validation, the teacher refers to the scores for the tasks or situations that fall within that standard. Bill Johnson's scores are 3, 3, and 2. Of course, there are many ways of aggregating scores into a summary score. Those who adhere to classical test theory would probably encourage the practice of averaging, because a numeric average tends to cancel out the random error associated with a score (Anastasi 1982). Some of those holding an outcome-based philosophy would no doubt make a case for considering an individual student's highest performance on a given standard as the summary validation that should be recorded. Such reasoning is founded on the assumption that the critical information a teacher should look for is evidence that a student can, in fact, meet the accepted level of performance. Given that a score of 3 is the accepted level of performance in a four-point rubric, any student who received at least one score of 3 should thus receive a summary score of 3.

Unfortunately, there is no clearly superior philosophy of assigning summary validations. In fact, the two positions described above represent two ends of a continuum. At one end is the numeric average, which calls for the use of as much information as possible in an unweighted fashion; in other words, one piece of information is counted as heavily as every other piece in the calculation of a numeric average. At the other end of the continuum is the single demonstration of competence, which recommends giving primary, even exclusive, weight to those tasks or situations designed to be culminating activities.

We suggest a compromise, albeit one that is strongly skewed toward the numeric average. Our method for assigning summary scores has four general rules:

1. Use as much information as possible, even information not recorded in the grade book. A summary score for a standard is an important piece of information for a student. It represents a teacher's final recommendation for a particular student on a particular standard. Therefore, a teacher should use all the information available to make that recommendation. If a teacher recalls that a student received a low score because of external factors such as illness or excused absences, these influences should be factored into the summary validation.

2. Weigh the various scores using sound criteria. Not all tasks and situations are equal. Some are more complex, some require more effort, some are culminating activities, some are developmental activities. A teacher should take these factors into consideration when assigning summary scores. For example, in Figure 4.1 the teacher might decide that the research project should be weighted much more heavily than the 15th century task and the two tests when assigning a summary score for the content standard

"Key people influence history" because the research project was a culminating activity in which students were to draw from everything they had learned in the unit.

3. Do not assign summary scores if adequate information is not available. Figure 4.1 shows that the teacher has not assigned summary scores for all standards for all students. To illustrate, consider the effective communication standard (see the EC column in Figure 4.1) and the records for the students Janie Pollock, John Kendall, and Joan Grady. None of these students has summary scores for the standard "Communicates in a variety of ways" because the teacher has concluded that she simply does not have enough information to assign a summary score, since some important tasks were not completed. Again, summary validations are important enough that they should not be assigned if significant amounts or types of information are lacking.

4. Consider the nature of the standards. A careful examination of the standards described in this text reveals at least two distinct types of standards: those focusing on *diversity* of knowledge or skill and those focusing on *consistency* of knowledge or skill. This difference is reflected in the summary rubrics. To illustrate, reconsider the summary rubric for the standard "communicates in a variety of ways." Recall from Chapter 2 that the standard deals with a student's ability to use a variety of communication methods, including oral reporting, reporting in written form, panel discussion, debate, and so on. The emphasis is obviously on the use of a range of communication mediums, and this emphasis is reflected in the summary rubric. Now consider the summary rubric for the standard "expresses ideas clearly," which is also from the effective communication category:

4 Consistently communicates information effectively by providing a clear main idea or theme with support that contains rich, vivid, and powerful detail.

3 Consistently communicates information by providing a clear main idea or theme with sufficient support and detail.

2 Sporadically communicates information by providing a clear main idea or theme with sufficient support and detail.

1 Rarely, if ever, communicates information by providing a clear main idea or theme with sufficient support and detail.

Here the focus is on consistent use of a proficiency in various situations. When assigning a summary validation for a standard that focuses on a range of knowledge or skill, the teacher needs access to information on the various types of knowledge or skills covered by the standard. When assigning a summary validation for a standard that focuses on consistency of knowledge or skill, the teacher needs access to information about that knowledge or skill exhibited at different times in different contexts.

As this discussion illustrates, no single philosophy is clearly superior in assigning summary validations. Teachers in a school or district should discuss their various philosophies and agree on at least a few common principles for assigning of summary validations to ensure that the validations can be interpreted uniformly.

Assessment at the School or District Level

The assessments made by individual teachers must ultimately be aggregated to obtain a composite picture of a student's performance on the various content standards and lifelong learning standards. This can be accomplished through multiple validations.

Multiple Validations

Multiple validations are assessments made over time, usually over the course of a semester or year. Obviously, no one teacher could cover all the content and lifelong learning standards a school or district might identify. Over time, though, assessments made by several teachers can provide a complete profile of a student's performance on all standards. A student's teachers individually assess various standards in their respective classes. In each class, the teacher provides summary validations (using the summary rubrics) for each student on each standard addressed in the class. Over the course of the semester, a student receives multiple summary validations for each standard. These multiple summary validations are referred to as "multiple validations," and they can be recorded in a Student Record. The complete Student Record contains a list of all the standards in each category. Figure 4.2 shows only a portion of the Student Record of a student named Bill Johnson; an entire blank Student Record is included in Chapter 9.

To illustrate the use of the Student Record form, consider the skilled information processing/consuming category in Figure 4.2. According to this Student Record, Bill Johnson has had summary validation scores submitted by two teachers. These are the multiple validations for this standard. The initials of the teachers who gave these validations are DB and AA. If we follow an outcome-based philosophy, each student is required to obtain a specific number of validations prior to graduation. For example, a district might decide that students must secure at least three validations in each standard prior to graduation. Given that the accepted level of performance in a four-point rubric is usually considered to be 3, each student then has to obtain at least three summary scores of 3 on each standard prior to graduation.

Of course, multiple validations can be used in systems that do not comply with an outcome-based philosophy. For example, multiple validations on a standard can be averaged to produce a metric that looks very much like a traditional grade-point average for each standard. Again, there is no one clearly superior philosophy about how to aggregate and report multiple validations. Consequently, a school or district must design a method that is consistent with its mission and goals.

Portfolios

Portfolios are an excellent adjunct or complement to multiple validations. They have received a great deal of attention in the past decade, particularly in the area of writing assessment (Belanoff and Dickson 1991). The original analogy for portfolio assessment was the artist's portfolio. Artists carry their completed, polished works in a portfolio that they show to prospective clients. In effect, artists use a portfolio to show what they can do, how versatile and good their work can be. Because writers, like most artists, produce tangible products, writing is perfectly suited to portfolio assessment. Hence, the field of writing instruction has seen the most extensive use of portfolios.

In a performance-based assessment system, portfolios include "physical evidence" of students' ability to meet the content standards and lifelong learning standards. It is quite common for standards to be collapsed into categories for portfolio assessment; that is, instead of providing evidence of the achievement of each separate standard in a category, a student provides physical evidence for the achievement of the group of standards in a category. For example, a student may select a written composition she feels is a particularly good illustration of her general competence in the effective communication category. She may also include in her portfolio a description of a community problem she undertook with a team of students to demonstrate her competence in the collaboration/cooperation category.

A school or district must make many important decisions about portfolio use:

- Should portfolios be constructed and displayed at every grade level or only at grade levels that represent transition points in school (e.g., end of primary school, end of upper elementary school, end of middle school, end of high school)?
- Should portfolios be used to assess the same standards that are assessed through multiple

FIGURE 4.2
Student Record
Part II

Student **Bill Johnson**

COMPLEX THINKING	Summary Validations				
1. Effectively translates issues and situations into manageable tasks that have a clear purpose.					
2. Effectively uses a variety of complex reasoning strategies.	4 AA				
SKILLED INFORMATION PROCESSING	**Summary Validations**				
1. Effectively interprets and synthesizes information.	3 DB	3 AA			
2. Effectively uses a variety of information-gathering techniques and information resources.					
3. Accurately assesses the value of information.					
4. Recognizes where and how projects would benefit from additional information.					
EFFECTIVE COMMUNICATION	**Summary Validations**				
1. Expresses ideas clearly.					
2. Effectively communicates with diverse audiences.					
3. Effectively communicates in a variety of ways.					
4. Effectively communicates for a variety of purposes.					
5. Creates high-quality products.					

validations, or should some standards or categories of standards be assessed only through portfolios and others only through multiple validations? Many schools and districts are thinking about assessing the areas of collaboration/cooperation and habits of mind through portfolios rather than multiple validations.

• How should multiple validations and portfolios be weighted? Can a student exhibit competence in one form and not in another? For example, could a student receive a satisfactory rating on her portfolio for a category of standards but not receive the designated number of multiple validations?

These are all serious issues that must be reconciled at least at the school level and most appropriately at the district level before a performance assessment system can be implemented.

*   *   *

The performance assessment movement has become a tremendous force in American education. In this book, we have described a system of performance assessment based on a powerful instructional framework, Dimensions of Learning. An important assumption underlying this book is that assessment and instruction must have a "hand in glove" relationship if they are to be successful. In using the Dimensions of Learning instructional model to develop the performance assessment system described here, we hope we have taken a first step in helping teachers and others successfully bring performance assessment into the classroom.

References

AASA. (1992). *Science for All Americans.* Washington, D.C.: American Association for the Advancement of Science.

Amabile, T. M. (1983). *The Social Psychology of Creativity.* New York: Springer-Verlag.

Anastasi, A. (1982). *Psychological Testing.* 5th ed. New York: Macmillan.

Archbald, D. A., and F. M. Newmann. (1988). *Beyond Standardized Tests.* Reston, Va.: National Association of Secondary School Principals.

Atwell, N. C. (1987). *In the Middle.* Portsmouth, N.H.: Heinemann

Baker, E. L., P. R. Aschbacher, D. Niemi, and E. Sato. (1992). *CRESST Performance: Assessment Models: Assessing Content Area Explanations.* Los Angeles: National Center for Research in Evaluation, Standards, and Student Testing, UCLA.

Baron, J. B. (1991). "Strategies for the Development of Effective Performance Exercises. *Applied Measurement in Education* 4: 305–318.

Belanoff, P., and M. Dickson. (1991). *Portfolios: Process and Product.* Portsmouth, N.H.: Boynton/Cook.

Berliner, D.C. (1979). "Tempus Educare". In *Research on Teaching,* edited by P. L. Peterson and H. J. Walberg. Berkeley, Calif.: McCutchan.

Bradley Commission on History in Schools. (1991). "Building a History Curriculum: Guidelines for Teaching History in Schools." In *Historical Literacy*, edited by P. Gagnon and the Bradley Commission on History in Schools. Boston: Houghton Mifflin.

Burns, M. (April 1986). "Teaching 'What to Do' in Arithmetic vs. Teaching 'What to Do and Why.' *Educational Leadership* 43, 7: 34–38.

Bush, G. (April 1991). "America 2000: The President's Education Strategy." Fact sheet. Washington, D.C.: Office of the Press Secretary, The White House.

Calkins, L. M. (1986). *The Art of Teaching Writing.* Portsmouth, N.H.: Heinemann.

Costa, A. L. (1991). "Toward a Model of Human Intellectual Functioning. In *Developing Minds: A Resource Book for Teaching Thinking,* revised edition, edited by A. Costa. Alexandria, Va.: Association for Supervision and Curriculum Development.

Costa, A. L., and R. J. Marzano. (1991). "Teaching the Language of Thinking." In *Developing Minds: A Resource Book for Teaching Thinking,* revised edition, edited by A. Costa. Alexandria, Va.: Association for Supervision and Curriculum Development.

Doyle, W. (1983). "Academic Work." *Review of Educational Research* 53, 2: 159–199.

Durst, R. K., and G. E. Newell. (1989). "The Uses of Function: James Britton's Category System and Research on Writing." *Review of Educational Research* 59, 4: 375–394.

Eisner, E. W. (February 1991). "What Really Counts in School." *Educational Leadership* 48, 5: 10–17.

Ennis, R. H. (1987). "A Taxonomy of Critical Thinking Dispositions and Abilities." In *Teaching Thinking Skills: Theory and Practice,* edited by J. Baron and R. Sternberg. New York: Freeman.

Fisher, C. W., N. Filby, R. S. Marliave, L. S. Cahen, M. M. Dishaw, J. E. Moore, and D. C. Berliner. (1978). *Teaching Behaviors, Academic Learning Time and Student Achievement.* San Francisco: Far West Laboratory of Educational Research and Development.

Fisher, C. W., and E. F. Hiebert. (1988). "Characteristics of Literacy Learning Activities in Elementary Schools." Paper presented at the annual meeting of the National Reading Conference, Tucson, Arizona.

Flavell, J. H. (1976). "Metacognitive Aspects of Problem Solving." In *The Nature of Intelligence,* edited by L. B. Resnick. Hillsdale, N.J.: Lawrence Erlbaum.

Herman, J. L., P. R. Aschbacher, and L. Winters. (1992). *A Practical Guide to Alternative Assessment.* Alexandria, Va.: Association for Supervision and Curriculum Development.

Jaques, E. (1985). "Development of Intellectual Capability." In *Essays on the Intellect,* edited by F. R. Link. Alexandria, Va.: Association for Supervision and Curriculum Development.

Johnson, D. W., and R. T. Johnson. (1987). *Learning Together and Alone.* 2nd ed. Englewood Cliffs, N.J.: Prentice-Hall.

Katz, L. G., and S. C. Chard. (1990). *Engaging Children's Minds: The Project Approach.* Norwood, N.J.: Ablex.

Kentucky Department of Education. (1991). *Learning Goals and Valued Outcomes.* Lexington, Ky.: Department of Education.

Macrorie, K. (1984). *Writing to Be Read.* Upper Montclair, N.J.: Boynton/Cook.

Marzano, R. J. (1992). *A Different Kind of Classroom: Teaching with Dimensions of Learning.* Alexandria, Va.: Association for Supervision and Curriculum Development.

Marzano, R. J., and A. L. Costa. (May 1988). "Question: Do Standardized Tests Measure Cognitive Skills? Answer: No." *Educational Leadership* 45, 8: 66–73.

Marzano, R. J., and J. S. Kendall. (1993). "The Systematic Identification and Articulation of Content Standards and Benchmarks: An Illustration Using Mathematics." Technical report. Aurora, Colo.: Mid-continent Regional Educational Laboratory.

Marzano, R. J., D. J. Pickering, D. E. Arredondo, G. J. Blackburn, R. S. Brandt, C. A. Moffett. (1992a). *Dimensions of Learning Teacher's Manual.* Alexandria, Va.: Association for Supervision and Curriculum Development.

Marzano, R.J., D. J. Pickering, D. E. Arredondo, G. J. Blackburn, R. S. Brandt, C. A. Moffett. (1992b). *Dimensions of Learning Trainer's Manual.* Alexandria, Va.: Association for Supervision and Curriculum Development.

Mitchell, R. (1992). *Testing for Learning: How New Approaches to Evaluation Can Improve American Schools.* New York: The Free Press.

Mullis, I. V. S., E. H. Owen, and G. W. Phillips. (1990). *America's Challenge: Accelerating Academic Achievement: A Summary of Findings from 20 Years of NAEP.* Princeton, N.J.: Educational Testing Service.

National Commission on Excellence in Education. (1983). *A Nation at Risk: The Imperative for Educational Reform.* Washington, D.C.: Government Printing Office.

National Commission on Testing and Public Policy. (1991). *From Gatekeeper to Gateway: Transforming Testing in America.* Chestnut Hill, Mass.: National Commission on Testing and Public Policy.

National Council of Teachers of Mathematics. (1989). *Curriculum and Evaluation Standards.* Reston, Va.: NCTM.

Paris, S. G., and B. K. Lindauer. (1982). "The Development of Cognitive Skills During Childhood." In *Handbook of Developmental Psychology,* edited by B. W. Wolman. Englewood Cliffs, N.J.: Prentice-Hall.

Paris, S. G., M. Y. Lipson, and K. K. Wixson. (July 1983). "Becoming a Strategic Reader." *Contemporary Educational Psychology* 8, 3: 293–316.

Paul, R., ed. (1990). *Critical Thinking: What Every Person Needs to Survive in a Rapidly Changing World.* Rohnert Park, Calif.: Center for Critical Thinking and Moral Critique.

Perkins, D. N. (Sept. 1984). "Creativity by Design." *Educational Leadership* 42, 1: 18–25.

Ravitch, D. (January 27, 1992). "National Education Standards." *Roll Call,* Education Policy Briefing, pp. 24–25.

Redding, N. (May 1991). "Assessing the Big Outcomes." *Educational Leadership* 49, 8: 49–53.

Resnick, L. B. (1987). *Education and Learning to Think.* Washington, D.C.: National Academy Press.

Secretary's Commission on Achieving Necessary Skills. (1991). *What Work Requires of Schools.* Washington, D.C.: U.S. Department of Labor.

Shanker, A. (June 17, 1992). "Coming to Terms on 'World Class Standards.'" *Education Week,* Special Report, p.S11.

Shavelson, R., G. Baxter, and J. Pine. (1992). "Performance Assessment: Political Rhetoric and Measurement Reality." *Educational Researcher* 21, 4: 22–27.

Shepard, L. A. (April 1989). "Why We Need Better Assessments." *Educational Leadership* 46, 7: 4–9.

Sizer, T. R. (1992). *Horace's School: Redesigning the American High School.* Boston: Houghton Mifflin.

Slavin, R. E. (1983). *Cooperative Learning.* New York: Longman.

Spady, W. G. (1988). "Organizing for Results: The Basis of Authentic Restructuring and Reform." *Educational Leadership* 46, 2: 4–8.

Tierney, R. J., M. A. Carter, L. F. Desai. (1991). *Portfolio Assessment in the Reading-Writing Classroom.* Norwood, Mass.: Christopher-Gordon Publishers.

Tucker, M. (June 17, 1992). "A New Social Compact for Mastery in Education." *Education Week,* Special Report, pp. S3–4.

Vosniadou, S., and W. F. Brewer. (Spring 1987). "Theories of Knowledge Restructuring and Development." *Review of Educational Research* 57, 1: 51–67.

Wiggins, G. (1989). "Teaching to the (Authentic) Task." *Educational Leadership* 46, 7: 41–47.

Wiggins, G. (Feb. 1991). "Standards, Not Standardization: Evoking Quality Student Work." *Educational Leadership* 48, 5: 18–25.

Zimmerman, B. J. (1990). "Self-Regulated Learning and Academic Achievement: The Emergence of a Social Cognitive Perspective." *Educational Psychology Review* 2: 173–201.

Part Two
Tools for Performance Assessment

5

Examples of Performance Tasks

This chapter contains sample performance tasks representing a variety of content areas and grade levels. Two tasks are presented for each of the complex reasoning processes from Dimensions 3 and 4. Those processes are:

Dimension 3 Reasoning Processes
- Comparing
- Classifying
- Induction
- Deduction
- Error analysis
- Constructing support
- Abstracting
- Analyzing perspectives

Dimension 4 Reasoning Processes
- Decision making
- Definitional investigation
- Historical investigation
- Projective investigation
- Problem solving
- Experimental inquiry
- Invention

For each task, the following information is presented:

1. The range of grade levels in which the task might be used. The following abbreviations are used to represent various grade levels:

- Pri. = primary
- U.E. = upper elementary
- Mid. = middle school
- J.H. = junior high school
- H.S. = high school

The tasks as presented in this chapter would, no doubt, have to be rewritten when used at a particular grade level. For example, a task that has a grade level range of Pri.–U.E. would probably have to be rewritten in a much simpler manner if used in the 1st grade and could be rewritten in a more complex manner if used in the 6th grade. Teachers can determine the language that's appropriate for their students.

2. The content standard the task is designed to assess. These tasks assume that a school or district has identified content standards that are to be assessed using performance assessment or that individual teachers are responsible for identifying the specific content standards they will cover.

3. The lifelong learning standards. These tasks assume that students are familiar with the various lifelong learning standards discussed in this book.

Finally, these tasks assume that students are familiar with the various complex reasoning processes from Dimensions 3 and 4.

Comparison Task

Grade level range: Mid.–H.S.

During this unit, we'll be learning about some of the general characteristics of governments. For instance, we'll learn that they all have "ways of providing services" and "policies to regulate behavior." So that you can use what you are learning, you'll be working with a few of your classmates in a small group to compare different kinds of governments. Your task will be to identify the similarities and differences among different sizes of governments, such as the rather large governments of countries and the much smaller governments of, say, school clubs.

During class, you'll be provided with the characteristics to use in a comparison matrix. You'll receive some suggestions about how to proceed, but the members of each group will determine the governments they want to compare. You must include the governments of at least two countries and the government of another group or organization you're familiar with—perhaps a club or even this school or classroom.

As you gain general knowledge about governments, you'll apply it to the specific items in your comparison matrix. It's important for your group to discuss the similarities and differences among the items in your matrix and to make sure each of you understands the characteristics we discuss in class.

Everyone in the group must have a copy of the group's matrix because after you have completed the matrix together, each of you will work individually to add one more item to the matrix. That item should be one that you know well, like your family or a club you belong to. I'm going to ask you to demonstrate your understanding of each characteristic of government by showing how your personal addition to the matrix is similar to and different from the other items in the matrix.

Each of you will hand in your completed matrix and another product of your choice that communicates what you've learned, not about individual governments, but about the more general concept of "government." We'll discuss in class some appropriate ways to communicate what you've learned. You'll be assessed on and provided rubrics for the following:

CONTENT STANDARD

Social Studies

1. Your understanding of the concept of government.

LIFELONG LEARNING STANDARDS

Complex Thinking: Comparison

1. Your ability to accurately identify the similarities and differences among types of governments.

Effective Communication

1. Your ability to communicate in a variety of ways.

Comparison Task

Grade level range: U.E.–Mid.

You have volunteered to help your local library with its literacy program. Once a week after school, you help people learn how to read. To encourage your students to learn, you tell them about the different kinds of literature you have read, including poems, biographies, mysteries, tall tales, fables, and historical novels. Select three types of literature and compare them, using general characteristics of literature that you think will help your students see the similarities and differences among the types of literature. Be ready to visually depict the comparison. You will be assessed on and provided rubrics for the following:

CONTENT STANDARDS

Language Arts

1. Your understanding of the general characteristics of literature.

2. Your knowledge of three selected types of literature.

LIFELONG LEARNING STANDARDS

Complex Thinking: Comparison

1. Your ability to specify appropriate items or elements to be compared.

Effective Communication

1. Your ability to communicate in a variety of ways.

Classification Task

Grade level range: U.E.–Mid.

Working in pairs, list as many insects as possible. Come up with a classification system that focuses on key characteristics of the insects and place the insects from your list in the appropriate categories. Do the same classification procedure two more times, but from the following perspectives:

• An exterminator (sample categories: insects found in homes, flying insects, crawling insects, insects commonly found in kitchens, insects that prefer dark basements)
• A frog (sample categories: insects that fly above water, that can swim, that would make a big meal, that would make a little meal).

You will have to consult various resources (materials in the classroom, peers, adults, and so on) to obtain the information necessary to classify the insects accurately. When you turn in your three classification systems, include a list of the resources you used and explain in a short paragraph which were most and least useful. Be ready to share with the class some interesting things you discovered as a result of doing these classifications. You will be assessed on and provided rubrics for the following:

CONTENT STANDARD

Science

1. Your understanding of the characteristics of insects.

LIFELONG LEARNING STANDARDS

Complex Thinking: Classification

1. Your ability to specify important defining characteristics of the categories.

2. Your ability to accurately sort the identified items or elements into the categories.

Effective Communication

1. Your ability to effectively use a variety of information-gathering techniques and information resources.

Classification Task

Grade level range: J.H.–H.S.

The accumulation of waste materials is a worldwide problem. Waste materials can be toxic, nontoxic, hard to get rid of, bulky, smelly, and so on. Imagine that your group of four has been selected to prepare a report for a task force of the federal government that classifies the various types of waste materials and proposes plans to address the problems. Using information gathered from our lessons and from other sources, classify the various types of waste materials. Then select one category of waste materials and present a plan for dealing with it. Your plan should be prepared as a research report to the government and should include the following elements:

1. Your classification of all waste materials and how you determined the categories.

2. An explanation of the effect your selected waste material has on the environment.

3. Your plan to deal with the waste material. This plan should contain references to the information sources you used and graphs and tables where appropriate.

4. The expected effect of your plan.

You will be assessed on and provided rubrics for the following:

CONTENT STANDARDS

Science

1. Your understanding of the effect of waste materials on the environment.

2. Your ability to prepare a research report.

LIFELONG LEARNING STANDARDS

Complex Thinking: Classification

1. Your ability to specify useful categories into which items or elements will be sorted.

2. Your ability to specify important defining characteristics of categories.

Effective Communication

1. Your ability to effectively interpret and synthesize information.

Induction Task

Grade level range: J.H.–H.S.

Observing human behavior can be very interesting and often very revealing. Select several different situations in which you can observe people and their behavior. For instance, you might choose to observe people at a mall, at a sports event, during lunch, or during the fifteen minutes before a movie begins. You must observe people in a given situation several different times, preferably with different people in the situation each time. Write down your observations, recording the date and time of each. This observation log should reflect your knowledge of the various categories of human behavior we have studied. What important conclusions can you make based on your observations? Describe the steps you took in coming to these conclusions. You will present your conclusions and defend them with your evidence to a panel of college students invited from the science department of the local university. You will be assessed on and provided rubrics for the following:

CONTENT STANDARD

Science—Physical and Social Sciences

1. Your understanding of the categories of human behavior.

LIFELONG LEARNING STANDARDS

Complex Thinking: Supported Induction

1. Your ability to identify elements (specific pieces of information or observations) from which to make inductions.

2. Your ability to make and articulate accurate conclusions (inductions) from the selected information or observations.

Effective Communication

1. Your ability to effectively communicate with diverse audiences.

Induction Task

Grade level range: U.E.–Mid.

Every week supermarkets spend lots of money on advertisements, with every supermarket claiming to have the lowest prices. Study the prices in recent ads from several supermarkets and find items that they all are advertising. Determine if any supermarket tends to have lower prices overall or if individual stores just have lower prices on some items and higher prices on others. Be careful to note the sizes and quantities (ounces, grams, pounds) connected with the costs.

After you have made this determination, notice how the advertisements are laid out and how the prices are displayed in the ads. Which items are featured? How are prices quoted differently in the ads? How does each supermarket go about making their products look less expensive?

Based on all of this analysis, come to at least two conclusions about the people who produce the advertisements for supermarkets and what they must think people want or will believe. Your conclusions might start with these sentence stems:

• People who do advertisements for supermarkets must think that people are . . .
• People who do advertisements for supermarkets must believe that . . .

Support each of your conclusions with evidence from the ads you examined. You must include evidence gained from your computations involving the prices and quantities in the ads.

You will present your findings in your small groups, consolidate your information, and prepare a report for the Channel 14 consumer expert when he visits our class next week. You will be assessed on and provided rubrics for the following:

CONTENT STANDARDS

Mathematics

1. Your ability to identify appropriate computations for a task.

2. Your ability to perform accurate computations.

3. Your ability to communicate the results of operations.

LIFELONG LEARNING STANDARDS

Complex Thinking: Supported Induction

1. Your ability to make, articulate, and support conclusions from information and observations.

Effective Communication

1. Your ability to effectively communicate in a variety of ways.

Deduction Task

Grade level range: J.H.–H.S.

During this unit, we will be watching clips from some of the legislative sessions carried on C-SPAN and taking a field trip to the Capitol. Find and describe a principle of democracy that is explicit or implicit in the way these legislative sessions are conducted. Specify the consequences of this principle by describing specific incidents you observed that can be explained in terms of the principle or can be shown to be a clear illustration of the principle. Observe another group to ascertain whether the group functions according to the same principle. Based on your observations, identify some logical consequences that might occur as a result of how the group is functioning in relation to that principle. At the end of this unit, you will present your

findings in a written report. You will be assessed on and provided rubrics for the following:

CONTENT STANDARD

Social Studies

1. Your understanding of democratic principles and practices.

LIFELONG LEARNING STANDARDS

Complex Thinking: Supported Deduction

1. Your ability to identify and articulate a deduction based on important or significant generalizations or principles implicit or explicit in information.

2. Your ability to identify and articulate logical consequences implied by the identified generalizations or principles.

Effective Communication

1. Your ability to effectively use a variety of information-gathering techniques and information resources.

Deduction Task

Grade level range: U.E.–Mid.

"An ounce of prevention is worth a pound of cure." "An apple a day keeps the doctor away." "Exercise—it's a matter of life or breath." We often hear sayings that identify the relationship between health and behavior, but for many people they are just rules to be ignored. The local health clinic has asked us to find a way to make these rules real to young people. We have to come up with specific examples that show how the rules apply. Select a rule or principle from the list I've provided and write down examples that will make the rule come alive. Then create a product the clinic might use to communicate to young people in our community this connection between a general rule of health and specific behaviors. Your product might be a poster, a flier, a radio spot, a television commercial, or anything else you think would reach young people. Before you begin working on your product, write down the criteria you want that product to fulfill. You will meet in small groups regularly to explain how you are working to create a product that fulfills your own personal criteria for a good product. We will present our ideas to the clinic. You will be assessed on and provided rubrics for the following:

CONTENT STANDARD

Health

1. Your understanding of the relationship between health and behavior.

LIFELONG LEARNING STANDARDS

Complex Thinking: Supported Deduction

1. Your ability to accurately interpret the generalizations or principles.

Effective Communication

1. Your ability to generate and pursue standards of performance.

Error Analysis Task

Grade level range: Pri.–U.E.

As we study community helpers, we will learn about the many things police officers do. You will be given time to work with a partner and make a list of everything the police do for the people in your community. Then, working alone or with a partner, you will watch at least three television shows about police and try to spot anything in these shows that differs from the way police work in real life. You and your partner should be ready to explain to the class the errors you saw on the television shows and your suggestions for making the shows more like real life. As we continue our learning about community helpers, you will be given a chance to share other errors that you notice. As you complete the task about the police, remember that you'll be assessed on these standards:

CONTENT STANDARD

Social Studies

1. Your understanding of how people in the community help us.

LIFELONG LEARNING STANDARDS

Complex Thinking: Error Analysis

1. Your ability to identify and articulate significant errors in information or processes.

2. Your ability to accurately describe how to correct errors.

Effective Communication

1. Your ability to effectively communicate with diverse audiences.

Error Analysis Task

Grade level range: J.H.–H.S.

Identify a recent disaster the local newspapers and television stations have been reporting on. Your task is to work with a partner to determine how the media convey information about the disaster to the public and identify specific examples of inaccurate information. You should include examples from a variety of newspapers, television broadcasts, eyewitness accounts, or interviews.

You must also identify specific examples of how these inaccuracies affected the people receiving the information and describe what might have been done to prevent such inaccuracies from being given to the public. Determine a way to present your findings to a member of the media, record that person's response, and share it with the other members of the class. You will be assessed on and provided rubrics for the following:

CONTENT STANDARD

Social Studies / Language Arts

1. Your understanding of your local media and how information is communicated to the public during a disaster.

LIFELONG LEARNING STANDARDS

Complex Thinking: Error Analysis

1. Your ability to identify and articulate significant errors in information or processes.

2. Your ability to accurately describe the effects of the errors on the information or process in which they originate.

Effective Communication

1. Your ability to use a variety of information-gathering techniques and information resources.

Constructing Support Task

Grade level range: U.E.–Mid.

As we study key conflicts and documents in American history, think about this famous statement: "The pen is mightier than the sword." Throughout the unit, you will periodically be given time to discuss with two other students whether you agree with this statement in the context of the conflicts and documents we are studying. Each time you discuss your views, keep a log of the reasons for and against supporting the statement. At the end of the unit, your group will reach consensus on how to view the statement. Each of you will then construct an argument supporting the statement or arguing against it. You must use specific historical examples in your argument. Be ready to present your argument to a group of people who will visit our classroom. This group includes newspaper reporters, authors, members of the military, and a legislator. You will be assessed on and provided rubrics for the following:

CONTENT STANDARDS

Social Studies

1. Your understanding of the effect of major conflicts on American history.

2. Your understanding of the effect of major written documents on American history.

LIFELONG LEARNING STANDARDS

Complex Thinking: Constructing Support

1. Your ability to provide sufficient and appropriate evidence for your claim.

Effective Communication

1. Your ability to effectively communicate with diverse audiences.

Constructing Support Task

Grade level range: J.H.–H.S.

A certain property near the school has been an empty lot for several years. Recently, land developers decided this property would be a good location for a gas station and, therefore, purchased the property. Many of people who live in this neighborhood have objected to the construction because the excavation process will disturb the habitat of the animals who live in the field. The land developers have now issued a statement saying that the animals will be able to adapt to the changes or will gradually move safely to new habitats.

You must decide whether you agree with their statement and find two other people who agree with you. Together, you will gather information about which animals dwell on the property and their ability or lack of ability to adapt to this change. You must present your position to people in the school and community by developing and distributing a flier providing supported evidence to help convince them that they should be involved in your cause. You must also prepare a petition form and gather names of the people who support you in your position. This petition, along with a brief presentation, will be presented to the city planning commission at the monthly planning meeting. You will be assessed on and provided rubrics for the following:

CONTENT STANDARD

Science and English

1. Your understanding of the concept of adaptation.

LIFELONG LEARNING STANDARDS

Complex Thinking: Constructing Support

1. Your ability to provide sufficient or appropriate evidence for the claim.

Effective Communication

1. Your ability to effectively communicate in a variety of ways.

Abstracting Task

Grade level range: Mid.– J.H.

For the next two weeks we will be studying American military conflicts of the past three decades, such as the Vietnam War and Operation Desert Storm. You will form teams of two and pretend that you and your partner will be featured in a newsmagazine television special about military conflict. Your team has been asked to help viewers understand the basic elements of these conflicts by relating them to a situation that has nothing to do with military conflict, but has the same basic elements. You are free to choose any nonmilitary situation you wish. In your explanation, the two of you must describe how the nonmilitary conflict fits each of the basic elements you identified in the military examples. You will prepare a report, with appropriate visuals, to present to the class in the way you would actually present it if you were doing your feature on the newsmagazine special. You will be assessed on and provided rubrics for the following:

CONTENT STANDARDS

Social Studies

1. Your understanding of the specific events surrounding the military conflicts.

2. Your understanding of the basic elements of military conflicts.

LIFELONG LEARNING STANDARDS

Complex Thinking: Abstracting

1. Your ability to identify a representative general or abstract form of the information.

2. Your ability to accurately articulate the relationship between the general or abstract pattern and the second set of information.

Effective Communication

1. Your ability to effectively use interpersonal communication skills in groups.

Abstracting Task

Grade level range: Pri.–U.E.

You have just finished reading three fairy tales that all have the same general pattern: characters overcoming a confrontation with an animal when the animal's intent is to harm the characters. Your task is to write a story that includes all the characteristics of a fairy tale and also uses this same general pattern. You will then present your story for publication in the school newspaper. You will be assessed on and provided rubrics for the following:

CONTENT STANDARD

English

1. Your understanding of the characteristics of a fairy tale.

LIFELONG LEARNING STANDARDS

Complex Thinking: Abstracting

1. Your ability to accurately articulate the relationship between the general or abstract pattern and the second set of information.

Effective Communication

1. Your ability to create a quality product.

Analyzing Perspectives Task

Grade level range: Mid.–J.H.

You will be provided with a number of provocative political ads focusing on current issues. Choose one of these, or any political ad to which you react emotionally, and write a letter to the editor describing your reaction to the ad. Be specific in identifying the techniques in the ad to which you reacted and the value underlying this reaction. Make a forceful "I believe" statement in your closing paragraph.

Next, imagine you are a someone who holds the opposing viewpoint and that you have just read the above letter and are now writing a letter in response. This letter must specifically define the opposing value and the reasoning behind it.

Finally, write a letter to a friend commenting on what you learned from this activity about the techniques used in advertisements to evoke emotional responses and what you learned about yourself and your own perspective. You will be assessed on and provided rubrics for the following:

CONTENT STANDARDS

Language Arts, Social Studies, Business

1. Your understanding of the techniques used in advertisements to evoke emotional responses.

2. Your ability to write business and social letters.

LIFELONG LEARNING STANDARDS

Complex Thinking: Analyzing Perspectives

1. Your ability to describe the reasoning or belief systems behind your value.

2. Your ability to describe the reasoning behind an opposing value.

Effective Communication

1. Your ability to effectively communicate for a variety of purposes.

Analyzing Perspectives Task

Grade level range: U.E.–Mid.

We have heard two speakers on the issue of schools in the United States requiring students to become fluent in both English and another language because we live in a global society. Examine your reaction to what one of the speakers said and use the top portion of the conflict clarification flow chart shown here to analyze your perspective. Then interview three individuals with different perspectives. Select one of these perspectives and fill out the bottom of the flow chart from this perspective. Your statements must be specific and your reasons should address the idea of living in a global society. You will be provided rubrics and assessed on the following:

CONTENT STANDARD

Social Studies, Foreign Language

1. Your ability to understand the implications of living in a global society.

LIFELONG LEARNING STANDARDS

Complex Thinking: Analyzing Perspectives

1. Your ability to describe the reasoning or belief systems behind a value.

2. Your ability to describe the reasoning behind an opposing value.

Self-Directed Learner

1. Your ability to seek different perspectives and consider choices before acting.

All students should be proficient in two languages.

I think this is _____

because _____

Others may think this is _____

because _____

By completing this flow chart I learned:

_____

_____

_____

Decision-Making Task

Grade level range: Mid.–J.H.

Select an influential person from the 15th or 16th century whose actions had important consequences. Determine the factors this person had to consider before taking those important actions. What alternatives were available to this person? Determine the goals that motivated the person in deciding to take the actions and the criteria the person probably applied in making the decision. What were the possible trade-offs in selecting one alternative over another? What were the risks and rewards, and how could either be measured? Without the benefit of hindsight, would you have made the same choice? Explain why or why not. As you study this decision, reflect on the kinds of history-making decisions that are made today. You can present your findings in oral or written form. You will be assessed on and provided rubrics for the following:

CONTENT STANDARD

Social Studies

1. How well you understand that history is influenced by the values and belief systems of influential people.

LIFELONG LEARNING STANDARDS

Complex Thinking: Decision Making

1. Your ability to identify appropriate and important alternatives to be considered.

2. Your ability to identify important and appropriate criteria for assessing alternatives.

Information Processing

1. Your ability to interpret and synthesize information.

Effective Communication

1. Your ability to serve a variety of purposes through communication.

Decision-Making Task

Grade level range: J.H.–H.S.

We will be studying Shakespeare and reading *Romeo and Juliet* during the upcoming unit. The focus of this unit, however, will be on the characteristics of classics within and across fields of study. We will initially concentrate on criteria for classics in literature, then evaluate *Romeo and Juliet* against these criteria using a decision matrix. You will independently add other pieces of modern literature to the matrix and determine which of them should qualify as potential classics. As we proceed through the unit, you may add to, revise, and delete criteria. You will hand in your completed matrix with summary conclusions.

In addition, working individually or in pairs, you will select any other field of interest where the term classic is used (for instance: cars, sports, arts, sciences). Set up a matrix to identify the "most classic" item in that field. You need to establish criteria for classics in that field (some of the criteria from the literature matrix apply) and consider specific choices for your classics (specific cars, pieces of art, experiments). Use your knowledge of the field or the information you learn during the project to select the "most classic" item. Be ready to report orally to the class the alternatives you considered in the matrix, the item that is the best example of a classic in a specific field, and how that item met each of the criteria in your matrix. You will be assessed on and provided rubrics for the following:

CONTENT STANDARDS

Science

1. Your understanding of the concept of "classic."

2. Your understanding of the criteria for literary classics.

LIFELONG LEARNING STANDARDS

Complex Thinking: Decision Making

1. Your ability to make a selection that adequately meets the decision criteria and answers the initial question.

Information Processing

1. Your ability to interpret and synthesize information.

Definitional Investigation Task

Grade level range: J.H.–H.S.

Although the term "Third World" is often used by newscasters, economists, and authors, its meaning is unclear to many people. There is no common understanding of precisely what the Third World is or where the term originated. In your small group, locate descriptions of, or allusions to, the Third World or to another regional term of your choice (e.g., underdeveloped nations, the Far East) that provide information or insights into the characteristics represented by the term and an explanation of why the term is used.

Construct a definition of the term and determine if its characteristics focus primarily on political, sociological, topographical, or religious distinctions. Use a consensus process to reach agreement on the definition. You will present your findings in a panel discussion format, so be prepared to defend your definition. You will be assessed on and provided rubrics for the following:

CONTENT STANDARD

Social Studies

1. Your ability to distinguish differing definitions of regions: those based primarily on politics, sociological elements, topography, religions, and so on.

LIFELONG LEARNING STANDARDS

Complex Thinking: Definitional Investigation

1. Your ability to construct a definition or detailed description of something for which there is no readily available or accepted definition.

2. Your ability to develop and defend a logical and plausible resolution to the confusion, uncertainty, or contradiction about the concept.

Information Processing

1. Your ability to search for and acquire information.

Definitional Investigation Task

Grade level range: U.E.–Mid.

Many similes and metaphors have been written that depict different people's understanding of the meaning of love. Working with a partner, examine the poetry you have been reading and identify at least eight similes and metaphors from different poets that depict their view of love.

Determine any agreements or contradictions that exist among the poets. Using this information, create a bumper sticker that you think depicts the meaning of love in a way that would be acceptable to all the poets whose work you've used. Present the bumper sticker to the students in your class along with a survey question asking whether they agree or disagree with the sentiments displayed on the bumper sticker and why.

After reviewing the completed surveys, report the results to the class. If some people did not agree with your bumper sticker, logically explain to the class why you think people did not agree. You will be provided with rubrics and assessed on the following:

CONTENT STANDARD

Language Arts

1. Your ability to identify similes and metaphors.

LIFELONG LEARNING STANDARDS

Complex Thinking: Definitional Investigation

1. Your ability to identify and explain the confusion, uncertainty, or contradiction surrounding a concept.

2. Your ability to develop and defend a logical and plausible resolution to the confusion, uncertainty, or contradiction surrounding a concept.

Effective Communication

1. Your ability to effectively communicate in a variety of ways.

Historical Investigation Task

Grade level range: Pri.–U.E.

There are competing theories about why dinosaurs became extinct. Most of the theories, however, recognize that it had something to do with the dinosaur's inability to adapt to the changing environment. For example, some say an "ice age" changed the environment. Others say a comet sent dust into the atmosphere, which blocked the sun's rays and thus changed the environment. Weigh the arguments of as many theories as you can find and determine which seems to be the most reasonable theory.

Then, using information from class, your textbook, and additional resources, work independently to write a report that answers the question "What happened to the dinosaurs?" You may construct your own theory by using a combination of ideas from several sources. Discuss the different theories you considered and then explain your theory and why it is the most reasonable theory in explaining the dinosaur's inability to adapt to a changing environment. You will be assessed on and provided rubrics for the following:

CONTENT STANDARD

Science

1. Your understanding of the role of adaptation in the survival of a species.

LIFELONG LEARNING STANDARDS

Complex Thinking: Historical Investigation

1. Your ability to construct an explanation for some past event for which an explanation is not readily available or accepted.

Self-Directed Learner

1. Your ability to seek different perspectives and consider choices before acting.

Historical Investigation Task

Grade level range: Mid.–H.S.

In recent years, controversy has arisen over the status of Christopher Columbus. Was he a hero or villain? As we study Columbus, we will read from a number of resources penned by different historians. In cooperative groups, choose at least two resources that describe conflicting reports of events that took place upon Columbus' "discovery" of the New World and during its settlement. Discuss the contradictions you find and try to determine why the historians reported events differently. Using the resources available, develop a clear explanation of the reasons for the contradictions or present a scenario that clears up the contradictions.

Your group will explain to the class why historians seem to report the same events differently and present a dramatization, panel, discussion, or debate that focuses on ideas for resolving the contradictions. We will then select those presentations that will be included in our Columbus Day assembly for the school. You will be assessed on and provided rubrics for the following:

CONTENT STANDARDS

Social Studies

1. Your understanding that recorded history is influenced by the perspective of the historian.

2. Your understanding of the events surrounding Columbus' "discovery" and settlement of the New World.

LIFELONG LEARNING STANDARDS

Complex Thinking: Historical Investigation

1. Your ability to identify and explain the confusion, uncertainty, or contradiction surrounding the past event.

2. Your ability to develop and defend a logical and plausible resolution to the confusion, uncertainty, or contradiction surrounding the past event.

Effective Communication

1. Your ability to communicate for a variety of purposes.

2. Your ability to communicate in a variety of ways.

Projective Investigation Task

Grade level range: Mid.–H.S.

We will be reading George Orwell's *1984,* which could be described as a work of projective investigation. We will also be studying what was happening in the world around time this book was written, the decade of the 1940s (Orwell wrote this book in 1948 and transposed the last two numbers to create the title *1984*).

First, working in small groups, your task is to select specific events, ideas, or trends from the 1940s and show how Orwell projected them into the future. You'll be given a chart on which you can graphically depict these connections.

Second, each person is to select a field of study that interests you (economics, science and technology, health care, fashion, sports, literature, the arts, politics, sociology) and select current events, ideas, and trends in that field, with an emphasis on areas where there is some controversy or disagreement.

Finally, using your knowledge of the field, construct a scenario for the future that makes sense and is a plausible extension of the present. Present your scenario in any way you wish (written prose or poetry, art form, oral or video presentation, etc.). In your presentation, clearly communicate your predictions and how they plausibly extend the present. You will be assessed on and provided rubrics for the following:

CONTENT STANDARDS

Interdisciplinary

1. Your understanding of the extent to which the present can inform the future.

2. Your depth of understanding of major events, ideas, and trends from a field of study.

LIFELONG LEARNING STANDARDS

Complex Thinking: Projective Investigation

1. Your ability to accurately identify what is already known or agreed upon about the future event.

2. Your ability to construct a scenario for some future event or hypothetical past event for which a scenario is not readily available or accepted.

Effective Communication

1. Your ability to express ideas clearly.

2. Your ability to effectively communicate in a variety of ways.

Projective Investigation Task

Grade level range: Pri.–Mid.

Imagine a world without music. Describe what life would be like in such a world. Identify the very specific roles that music serves now and describe how these roles would change in a world without music. Paint a vivid picture so we can feel what it would be like to live in that world. Choose whatever form of communication (essay, oral presentation, video, etc.) seems best suited to your purpose and will allow you to produce a quality product.

CONTENT STANDARD

Music

1. Your understanding of the role of music in everyday life.

LIFELONG LEARNING STANDARDS

Complex Thinking: Projective Investigation

1. Your ability to identify and explain the confusion, uncertainty, or contradiction surrounding a future event.

Effective Communication

1. Your ability to create quality products.

Problem-Solving Task

Grade level range: Pri.–U.E.

We have been studying two shapes, circles and squares. We will be taking a walk through the school neighborhood to look at the shapes of buildings, people, and cars. Then you will draw a picture of the school neighborhood, your neighborhood, or a city. Include buildings, people, and cars. You cannot use any circles or squares in your drawing. As you work, ask a friend to keep checking your picture to see if you have used either of these shapes.

When you're finished, I will ask some of you to explain what you learned about shapes and about how shapes are used in our lives every day. When you turn in your picture, I will look to see if you used any circles and squares. While you are working, I will ask you to explain to me, using the words for the shapes we have studied, what you are learning by drawing this picture. Remember, we have discussed how we solve problems. I will also ask you to explain what makes this assignment hard. I will show you examples of what I will be looking for in your pictures and in your answers to my questions.

CONTENT STANDARDS

Math

1. How well you understand the importance of shapes in our world.

2. How well you can recognize circles and squares.

LIFELONG LEARNING STANDARDS

Complex Thinking: Problem Solving

1. How well you can identify things that keep you from solving a problem.

Effective Communication

1. How well you can express what you are thinking so everyone understands you.

Problem-Solving Task

Grade level range: Mid.–H.S.
Some people are calling for mandatory drug testing in many job settings and other areas of life (for example, in sports). Yet mandatory testing is rare. What is behind the call for mandatory drug testing? That is, what benefits are there to mandatory drug testing?

Imagine that you have been hired by a group that supports mandatory drug testing to solve the problems that have prevented mandatory testing from becoming a more widespread reality. You are also charged with designing a campaign that will encourage more people to institute mandatory drug testing. Use a variety of resources to learn about the issue and plan your presentation, which you will make to a group of your choice. You will be assessed on and provided rubrics for the following:

CONTENT STANDARDS

Science, Social Studies

1. Your understanding of the effects of drug use on society.

2. Your understanding of the interplay of individual rights and societal protection.

LIFELONG LEARNING STANDARDS

Complex Thinking: Problem Solving

1. Your ability to accurately identify viable and important alternatives for overcoming the constraints or obstacles.

Effective Communication

1. Your ability to communicate for a variety of purposes.

2. Your ability to create quality products.

Experimental Inquiry Task

Grade level range: J.H.–H.S.
Identify interesting behavior you have noticed while riding in an elevator. Explain this phenomenon using accepted sociological and psychological principles. Based on your understanding of the principles involved, make a prediction that can be tested. Set up an experiment that will test your prediction and help explain the principles you have discovered. Describe whether the experiment proved or disproved your hypothesis and whether the principles you've described still hold true. When you present your findings to the class, you need to support your oral presentation with a demonstration. You will be assessed on and provided rubrics for the following:

CONTENT STANDARD

Social Sciences

1. Your ability to analyze how individuals and groups react in certain social situations.

LIFELONG LEARNING STANDARDS

Complex Thinking: Experimental Inquiry

1. Your ability to accurately explain the phenomenon initially observed using facts, concepts, or principles.

Effective Communication

1. Your ability to set up and carry out an experiment that tests your prediction.

Experimental Inquiry Task

Grade level range: U.E.–Mid.

We have been learning about climate, culture, and topography. We have also been discussing why people live in certain areas. Although some people have no choice about where they live, other people do. Why do you think people choose to live here in our state? Why do you think some people say they would not like to live here? Choose one of these two questions and write three possible reasons (hypotheses) people might choose to live or not live here. Come up with one possible reason that relates to climate (for example, "People live here because they prefer low humidity and snow"), one that relates to culture (for example, "People live here because of the sports and leisure activities"), and one that relates to topography (for example, "People don't live here because it is so far from an ocean).

Select one of your hypotheses and set up an experiment to test it. Be ready to share your conclusions with the class in an oral report. Your report should include an explanation of how you arrived at your hypothesis, a description of your experiment, and an explanation of how the results supported or did not support your hypothesis. You will be assessed on and provided rubrics for the following:

CONTENT STANDARD

Social Studies / Science

1. Your understanding of the concepts of culture, climate, and topography.

LIFELONG LEARNING STANDARDS

Complex Thinking: Experimental Inquiry

1. Your ability to accurately explain a phenomenon (i.e, that of people choosing to live or not to live here) with appropriate and accepted facts, concepts, or principles (the concepts of culture, climate, and topography).

Effective Communication

1. Your ability to express ideas clearly.

Invention Task

Grade level range: Mid.–H.S.

Pretend the people in your group are mad scientists who enjoy inventing new things. A weather forecaster tells you that human hair can be used to measure humidity. When the air is moist, hair expands; When the air is dry, hair shrinks. The change in length, and therefore humidity, is measured using an instrument called a hair hygrometer.

You decide you will invent a new instrument that can be used to measure some other aspect(s) of weather we will be studying. As you work on your invention, try it out and find ways to make it the best it can be (unique, accurate, easy to use, durable, attractive, etc.). Describe your invention in a written report with diagrams of the invention, or turn in a model of your invention and the results you obtained after using the invention for at least three real-life measurements. In the report, describe at least one difficulty you had in developing your invention and then describe how you kept yourself on task when faced with that difficulty. You will be assessed on and provided rubrics for the following:

CONTENT STANDARD

Science

1. Your understanding of the major aspects of weather.

LIFELONG LEARNING STANDARDS

Complex Thinking: Invention

1. Your ability to make detailed and important revisions in the initial process or product.

Self-Directed Learner

1. Your ability to push your limits and persevere when facing difficult situations.

Invention Task

Grade level range: Pri.–U.E.

We have been studying characteristics that help animals adapt to their environment. Your task now is to select an animal you're familiar with and figure out a way to improve that animal by changing one or more of its characteristics so that it could adapt even better to its environment. Draw a picture of your new and improved animal and be ready to explain exactly how your change(s) would help it adapt. Be ready to present your picture and explanation to the class. You will be assessed on and provided rubrics for the following:

CONTENT STANDARD

Science

1. Your understanding of the concept of adaptation.

LIFELONG LEARNING STANDARDS

Complex Thinking: Invention

1. Your ability to identify rigorous and important standards or criteria the invention will meet.

Effective Communication

1. Your ability to express your ideas clearly.

6

Rubrics for Specific Tasks or Situations

Rubrics for Content Standards

A. Generic Rubric for Declarative Standards

4   Demonstrates a thorough understanding of the generalizations, concepts, and facts specific to the task or situation and provides new insights into some aspect of this information.

3   Displays a complete and accurate understanding of the generalizations, concepts, and facts specific to the task or situation.

2   Displays an incomplete understanding of the generalizations, concepts, and facts specific to the task or situation and has some notable misconceptions.

1   Demonstrates severe misconceptions about the generalizations, concepts, and facts specific to the task or situation.

Note that this generic rubric must be rewritten to include the specifics of the information in a declarative standard, as in the example shown here:

Mathematics Example (4th Grade): Understands how basic geometric shapes are used in the planning of well-organized communities.

4   Demonstrates a thorough understanding of how basic geometric shapes are used in the planning of well-organized communities and provides new insights into some aspect of their use.

3   Displays a complete and accurate understanding of how geometric shapes are used in the planning of well-organized communities.

2   Displays an incomplete understanding of how basic geometric shapes are used in the planning of well-organized communities and has some notable misconceptions about their use.

1   Has severe misconceptions about how basic geometric shapes are used in the planning of well-organized communities.

B.   Generic Rubric for Procedural Standards

4   Demonstrates mastery over the strategy or skill specific to the task or situation. Can perform the strategy or skill without error and with little or no conscious effort.

3   Carries out the strategy or skill specific to the task or situation without significant error.

2   Makes a number of errors when performing the strategy or skill specific to the task or situation but can complete a rough approximation of it.

1   Makes many critical errors when performing the strategy or skill specific to the task or situation.

Note that this generic rubric must be rewritten to include the specifics of the information in a procedural standard, as in the example shown here:

Mathematics Example (4th Grade): Accurately and efficiently converts measurements from the metric system into the English system.

4   Demonstrates mastery over the process of converting measurements from the metric system into the English system. Can perform the process without error and with little or no conscious effort.

3   Carries out the process of converting measurements from the metric system into the English system without significant error.

2   Makes significant errors when converting measurements from the metric system to the English system but can complete a rough approximation of the process.

1   Makes many critical errors when converting measurements from the metric system to the English system.

Rubrics for Complex Thinking Standards

A.   Effectively translates issues and situations into meaningful tasks that have a clear purpose.

4   Translates the issue or situation into a well-articulated task that has clearly defined goals and involves clearly identifiable complex reasoning processes. Anticipates and articulates difficulties the task might present.

3   Translates the issue or situation into a task that has clearly defined goals and involves clearly identifiable complex reasoning processes.

2   Translates the issue or situation into a task that has poorly defined goals.

1   Makes an attempt to translate the issue or situation into a task but provides no understandable description of the nature or purpose of the task or makes no attempt to translate the issue or situation into a task.

B.   Effectively uses a variety of complex reasoning strategies.

REASONING STRATEGY 1: COMPARISON
Comparison involves describing the similarities and differences between two or more items. The process includes three components that can be assessed:

a.   Selects appropriate items to compare.

b.   Selects appropriate characteristics on which to base the comparison.

c.   Accurately identifies the similarities and differences among the items, using the identified characteristics.

a.   Selects appropriate items to compare.

4   Selects items that are extremely suitable for addressing the basic objective of the comparison and that show original or creative thinking.

3   Selects items that provide a means for successfully addressing the basic objective of the comparison.

2   Selects items that satisfy the basic requirements of the comparison, but create some difficulties for completing the task.

1   Selects items that are inappropriate to the basic objective of the comparison.

b.   Selects appropriate characteristics on which to base the comparison.

4   Selects characteristics that encompass the most essential aspects of the items and present a unique challenge or provide an unusual insight.

3   Selects characteristics that provide a vehicle for meaningful comparison of the items and address the basic objective of the comparison.

2   Selects characteristics that provide for a partial comparison of the items and may include some extraneous characteristics.

1   Selects characteristics that are trivial or do not address the basic objective of the comparison. Selects characteristics on which the items cannot be compared.

c.   Accurately identifies the similarities and differences among the items, using the identified characteristics.

4   Accurately assesses all identified similarities and differences for each item on the selected characteristic. Additionally, the student provides inferences from the comparison that were not explicitly requested in the task description.

3   Accurately assesses the major similarities and differences among the identified characteristics.

2   Makes some important errors in identifying the major similarities and differences among the identified characteristics.

1   Makes many significant errors in identifying the major similarities and differences among the identified characteristics.

REASONING STRATEGY 2: CLASSIFICATION

Classification involves organizing items into categories based on specific characteristics. The process includes four components that can be assessed:

a.   Selects significant items to classify.

b.   Specifies useful categories for the items.

c.   Specifies accurate and comprehensive rules for category membership.

d.   Accurately sorts the identified items into the categories.

a.   Selects significant items to classify.

4   Specifies the items to be classified and selects significant items that present some interesting challenge in classification.

3   Selects significant items for classification that present some challenge in classification.

2   Selects items of little significance or presents a routine sorting problem.

1   Selects trivial items or items that have no relationship to the task.

b. Specifies useful categories for the items.

4   Creates categories that provide a useful way of looking at the items at an unusual level of depth.

3   Creates categories that focus on the significant characteristics of the items.

2   Creates categories that provide for some analysis of the items but may not include all the important characteristics of the items.

1   Creates categories that address only trivial aspects of the items.

c. Specifies accurate and comprehensive rules for category membership.

4   Provides a clear and complete specification of the defining characteristics of each category. Describes the defining characteristics in such a way as to provide a unique or unusual way of looking at the items.

3   Clearly specifies the defining characteristics of the categories and addresses any questions of overlap in characteristics.

2   Describes the defining characteristics of categories in a way that results in some overlap or confusion between categories, or describes characteristics that are unrelated to the rules for category membership.

1   Identifies characteristics that do not accurately describe the categories.

d. Accurately sorts the identified items into the categories.

4   Correctly sorts each of the items into the categories and describes the extent to which each item has the characteristics ascribed to the categories. Describes insights gained during the sorting process.

3   Correctly sorts each of the items into the categories and, when appropriate, describes the extent to which each item has the characteristics ascribed to the categories.

2   Makes some errors in assigning items to their appropriate categories, or does not describe the extent to which each item has the characteristics of the category, when it is clearly appropriate for the task.

1   Makes frequent and significant errors in assigning items to categories and does not show how the items have the characteristics of their assigned categories.

REASONING STRATEGY 3: INDUCTION

Induction involves creating a generalization from implicit or explicit information and then describing the reasoning behind the generalization. The process includes three components that can be assessed:

a.   Identifies elements (specific pieces of information or observations) from which to make inductions.

b.   Interprets the information from which inductions are made.

c.   Makes and articulates accurate conclusions (inductions) from the selected information or observations.

a.   Identifies elements (specific pieces of information or observations) from which to make inductions.

4   Clearly and accurately identifies all relevant information from which to make inductions. The type of information selected reflects creative insight and a careful analysis of the situation.

3   Specifies all relevant information from which to make inductions. Selects information that is important to the general topic.

2   Includes some information that is not important to the induction or does not accurately identify the important information from which the induction(s) could be made.

1   Selects unimportant or trivial information for the induction.

b.   Interprets the information from which inductions are made.

4   Provides accurate interpretations that illustrate insight into the information from which they were made. The interpretations reflect a study of or a familiarity with the particulars of the topic.

3   Provides interpretations that, with few exceptions, are valid and say something important about the topic.

2   Provides some interpretations that are based on significant misunderstandings of the subject matter.

1   Significantly misinterprets the information. Makes interpretations that have no bearing on the area or are clearly illogical.

c.   Makes and articulates accurate conclusions (inductions) from the selected information or observations.

4   Draws conclusions that reflect clear and logical links between the information or observations and the interpretations made from them. The rationale for the interpretations shows a thoughtful and accurate attention to the process of induction.

3   Presents conclusions that, with few exceptions, follow logically from the selected information or observations.

2   Presents some conclusions that reflect erroneous interpretations made from the information or observations.

1   Draws many erroneous conclusions from the selected information or observations and cannot satisfactorily describe the rationale behind the conclusions.

REASONING STRATEGY 4: DEDUCTION

Deduction involves identifying implicit or explicit generalizations or principles (premises) and then describing their logical consequences. The process includes three components that can be assessed:

a.   Identifies and articulates a deduction based on important and useful generalizations or principles implicit or explicit in the information.

b.   Accurately interprets the generalizations or principles.

c.   Identifies and articulates logical consequences implied by the identified generalizations or principles.

a.   Identifies and articulates a deduction based on important and useful generalizations or principles implicit or explicit in the information.

4   Selects generalizations or principles that show extreme insight into the topic.

3   Selects important generalizations or principles that contribute to the understanding of the material being studied.

2   Selects generalizations or principles that generally relate to the information available but that may not have significant explanatory power.

1   Selects generalizations or principles that do not have significant bearing on the material and do not contribute to the understanding of the subject.

b.   Accurately interprets the generalizations or principles.

4   Demonstrates an understanding of the generalizations or principles that is not only accurate but provides a unique perspective on the topic.

3   Demonstrates an understanding of the generalizations or principles that is accurate and contributes to an understanding of the topic.

2   Demonstrates a somewhat inaccurate understanding of the generalizations or principles.

1   Demonstrates an incorrect understanding or interpretation of the generalizations or principles.

c.   Identifies and articulates logical consequences implied by the identified generalizations or principles.

4   Accurately identifies logical conclusions implied by the generalizations or principles. Recognizes more subtle inferences that could have important effects on the subject area.

---

3   With few errors, accurately identifies the consequences of the generalizations or principles. The consequences relate closely to the subject area and are worthwhile subjects for discussion.

2   Accounts for important consequences of the generalizations or principles, but identifies consequences that may not be germane to the topic; or makes logical errors in identifying the consequences.

1   Identifies consequences that have little significance and are not logical or germane to the topic.

REASONING STRATEGY 5: ERROR ANALYSIS

Error analysis involves identifying and describing specific types of errors in information or processes. It includes three components that can be assessed:

a.   Identifies and articulates significant errors in information or in a process.

b.   Accurately describes the effects of the errors on the information or process.

c.   Accurately describes how to correct the errors.

a.   Identifies and articulates significant errors in information or in a process.

4   Accurately identifies all errors in the information or process under study and makes clear why the points identified are errors. Also identifies subtle but important errors that are difficult to recognize.

3   Accurately identifies all critical errors in the information or process under study and makes clear why the points identified are errors.

2   Fails to recognize some important errors or identifies some points that are not errors.

1   Recognizes only insignificant errors or mistakes valid points for errors.

b.   Accurately describes the effects of the errors on the information or process.

4   Provides an accurate analysis of the effects of the errors, including a complete description of the ramifications of the errors beyond the most obvious levels of impact.

3   Provides an accurate analysis of the effects of the errors, omitting few details.

2   Describes the effects of the errors, but omits some important consequences; or does not accurately describe all the effects of the errors.

1   Does not correctly assess the effects of the errors, or describes effects that do not exist.

c. Accurately describes how to correct the errors.

4   Provides a highly thoughtful or creative approach for correcting the errors.

3   Provides a workable way of correcting the errors. The response addresses the major concerns raised by the errors.

2   Provides an approach for correcting the errors. The approach addresses some of the major errors, though it may not be the best or most appropriate response to the situation.

1   Does not accurately describe how to correct the errors.

REASONING STRATEGY 6: CONSTRUCTING SUPPORT

Constructing support involves developing a well-articulated argument for or against a specific claim. The process includes three components that can be assessed:

    a.   Accurately identifies a claim that requires support rather than a fact that does not require support.

    b.   Provides sufficient or appropriate evidence for the claim.

    c.   Adequately qualifies or restricts the claim.

a. Accurately identifies a claim that requires support rather than a fact that does not require support.

4   Accurately identifies a claim that requires support. The identified claim has been mistaken by many others for a fact that requires no support.

3   Accurately identifies a claim that requires support and does not confuse the claim with any other information.

2   Identifies a claim that requires support but may mistakenly include information that does not require support.

1   Identifies information that does not require support and fails to identify a claim that should have support.

b. Provides sufficient or appropriate evidence for the claim.

4   Presents a clear and accurate treatment of all available evidence that addresses the central point of the claim. Considers what evidence is missing and how it should affect an evaluation of the claim.

3   With no major errors, presents all relevant evidence needed to support the claim.

2   Provides evidence for the claim, but may not address all necessary aspects.

1   Fails to provide convincing evidence for the claim.

c. Accurately qualifies or restricts the claim.

4   Provides careful and reasoned qualifications or restrictions for the claim in such a way that the argument provides a unique perspective on the claim.

3   Provides accurate qualifications or restrictions for the claim, with the result being a well-defended claim.

2   Qualifies or restricts the claim, but leaves out important aspects of the qualifications or restrictions.

1   Does not address qualifications or restrictions for the claim.

REASONING STRATEGY 7: ABSTRACTING

Abstracting involves identifying and explaining how the abstract pattern in one situation or set of information is similar to or different from the abstract pattern in another situation or set of information. The process includes three components that can be assessed:

a.   Identifies a significant situation or meaningful information that is useful as a subject for the abstracting process.

b.   Identifies a representative general or abstract pattern for the situation or information.

c.   Accurately articulates the relationship between the general or abstract pattern and another situation or set of information.

a. Identifies a significant situation or meaningful information that is useful as a subject for the abstracting process.

4   Identifies a situation or information that provides a rich source of material for the process of abstracting. The selected information is not commonly used in abstracting tasks but has a pattern that could be quite powerful when abstracted.

3   Identifies significant information that also has a pattern that lends itself to the abstracting process.

2   Identifies information that seems unimportant but does have a pattern that can be used in the abstracting process.

1   Identifies trivial information having no identifiable pattern that can be used in the abstracting process.

b. Identifies a representative general or abstract pattern for the information.

4   Identifies a general or abstract pattern that provides unusual or provocative insights into the information under study. The pattern furnishes the means for seeing other material from a unique perspective.

3   Constructs a general or abstract pattern that accurately represents the information from which it came.

2   Creates a general or abstract pattern that may not be a completely accurate representation of the information or situation from which it was drawn but does focus on its most important elements.

1   Does not create a general or abstract pattern that accurately represents the information or situation selected.

c. Accurately articulates the relationship between the general or abstract pattern and another situation or set of information.

4   Demonstrates creativity in the selection of another situation or set of information that contains a similar general or abstract form. The situation or information is important and provides a very good subject for analysis.

3   Correctly identifies another situation or set of information that contains the essential characteristics of the general or abstract form and provides a worthwhile subject for study.

2   Identifies another situation or set of information that does perfectly match the general or abstract form but has some similarities.

1   Selects another situation or set of information that does not conform in any way to the general or abstract pattern identified.

REASONING STRATEGY 8: ANALYZING PERSPECTIVES

Analyzing perspectives involves considering one perspective on an issue and the reasoning behind it as well as an opposing perspective and the reasoning behind it. The process includes three components that can be assessed:

a. Identifies an issue on which there is disagreement.

b. Identifies one position on the issue and the reasoning behind it.

c. Identifies an opposing position and the reasoning behind it.

a. Identifies an issue on which there is disagreement.

4   Identifies and articulates implicit points of disagreement that are not obvious but are the underlying cause of conflict.

3   Identifies and articulates explicit points of disagreement that cause conflict.

2   Identifies and articulates issues that are not points of disagreement as important issues of disagreement.

1   Ignores explicit and implicit points of disagreement.

b. Identifies one position on the issue and the reasoning behind it.

4   Articulates a detailed position and the reasoning behind it and, if a strong line of reasoning does not underlie the position, articulates the errors or holes in the reasoning.

3   Articulates a position and the basic reasoning underlying the position. Does not address or incompletely addresses the errors or holes in the reasoning.

2   Articulates a position but does not present a clear line of reasoning behind it.

1   Does not articulate a clear position.

c. Identifies an opposing position and the reasoning behind it.

4   Articulates a detailed opposing position and the reasoning behind it. If a strong line of reasoning does not underlie the position, articulates the errors or holes in the reasoning.

3   Articulates an opposing position and the basic reasoning underlying it. Does not address or incompletely addresses the errors or holes in the reasoning.

2   Articulates an opposing position but does not present a clear line of reasoning behind it.

1   Does not articulate a clear opposing position.

REASONING STRATEGY 9: DECISION MAKING

Decision making involves selecting among apparently equal alternatives. It includes four components that can be assessed:

a. Identifies important and appropriate alternatives to be considered.

b. Identifies important and appropriate criteria for assessing the alternatives.

c. Accurately identifies the extent to which each alternative possesses each criteria.

d. Makes a selection that adequately meets the decision criteria and answers the initial decision question.

a. Identifies important and appropriate alternatives to be considered.

4   Presents a comprehensive list of the most important possible alternatives and describes each in detail.

3   Identifies alternatives that represent most of the important possible alternatives.

2   Identifies some alternatives that are important and others that are not.

1   Selects alternatives that are clearly not relevant to the decision.

b. Identifies important and appropriate criteria for assessing the alternatives.

4   Clearly identifies the criteria by which the identified alternatives will be assessed. The criteria reflect an unusually thorough understanding of the nature of the decision task.

3   Clearly identifies the criteria by which the identified alternatives will be assessed. With no significant exceptions, the criteria are important to the decision task.

2   Identifies some important criteria by which the identified alternatives will be assessed. However, some important criteria are omitted, or criteria are included that may not be important to the decision task.

1   Identifies few or no criteria that are relevant to the decision task.

c. Accurately identifies the extent to which each alternative possesses each criteria.

4   Provides a thorough, fully developed assessment of each alternative based upon the criteria. Exceeds the demands of the decision task by comparing and contrasting the alternatives to provide greater insights.

3   Presents an accurate assessment of the extent to which the alternatives possess the identified criteria.

2   Does not completely address all the criteria; or applies all appropriate criteria to the alternatives but is not completely accurate in assessing how well the criteria have been met.

1   Does not address the extent to which the alternatives meet the criteria or is inaccurate is assessing how well the alternatives meet the criteria.

d. Makes a selection that adequately meets the decision criteria and answers the initial decision question.

4   Selects an alternative that meets or exceeds the criteria and that represents a well-supported answer to the initial decision question. Provides a useful discussion of issues and insights that arose during the selection process.

3   Successfully answers the decision question by selecting an alternative that meets or exceeds established criteria.

2   Selects an alternative that does not entirely conform to the student's assessment of the alternatives.

1   Makes a selection that does not appear reasonable or cannot be justified by the student's evaluation of the alternatives.

REASONING STRATEGY 10: INVESTIGATION

Investigation is a process involving close examination and systematic inquiry. There are three basic types of investigation:

- *Definitional Investigation:* Constructing a definition or detailed description of a concept for which such a definition or description is not readily available or accepted.

- *Historical Investigation:* Constructing an explanation for some past event for which an explanation is not readily available or accepted.

- *Projective Investigation:* Constructing a scenario for some future event or hypothetical past event for which a scenario is not readily available or accepted.

Each type of investigation includes three components that can be assessed:

a. Accurately identifies what is already known or agreed upon about the concept (definitional investigation), the past event (historical investigation), or the future event (projective investigation).

b. Identifies and explains the confusions, uncertainties, or contradictions about the concept (definitional investigation), the past event (historical investigation), or the future event (projective investigation).

c. Develops and defends a logical and plausible resolution to the confusions, uncertainties, or contradictions about the concept (definitional investigation), the past event (historical investigation), or the future event (projective investigation).

a. **Accurately identifies what is already known or agreed upon about the concept (definitional investigation), the past event (historical investigation), or the future event (projective investigation).**

4 Presents a thorough and correct account of what is already known. Supplies information that may not be commonly known, but that has some bearing on the topic being studied.

3 Presents an accurate account, with no important omissions, of what is already known or agreed upon about the topic being studied.

2 Presents information on what is already known or agreed upon about the topic being studied; however, the information may not be complete in all particulars, or the student may introduce some inaccuracies.

1 Presents little or no accurate and important information about what is already known or agreed upon about the topic.

b. **Identifies and explains the confusions, uncertainties, or contradictions about the concept (definitional investigation), the past event (historical investigation), or the future event (projective investigation).**

4 Identifies the important confusions, uncertainties, or contradictions surrounding the topic. Brings to light misconceptions or confusions that are commonly overlooked.

3 Identifies, with no important errors, significant confusions, uncertainties, or contradictions surrounding the topic.

2 Identifies confusions, uncertainties, or contradictions associated with the topic. The problems identified include some, but not all, of the most critical issues.

    1   Fails to accurately identify any important confusions, uncertainties, or contradictions surrounding the topic.

c. Develops and defends a logical and plausible resolution to the confusions, uncertainties, or contradictions about the concept (definitional investigation), the past event (historical investigation), or the future event (projective investigation).

    4   Provides a logical and well-developed resolution to the confusions, uncertainties, or contradictions. The resolution reflects creative thinking as well as thoughtful attention to the details of the problem.

    3   Presents a clear resolution to the problems associated with the concept. The resolution is a logical and plausible outcome of the investigation.

    2   Develops and presents a resolution to the problems associated with the concept. The resolution is satisfactory, but lacks thorough treatment and accuracy.

    1   Presents an unsubstantiated and implausible resolution to the confusions, uncertainties, or contradictions.

REASONING STRATEGY 11: PROBLEM SOLVING

Problem solving involves developing and testing a method or product for overcoming obstacles or constraints to reach a desired outcome. It includes four components that can be assessed:

    a. Accurately identifies constraints or obstacles.

    b. Identifies viable and important alternatives for overcoming the constraints or obstacles.

    c. Selects and adequately tries out alternatives.

    d. If other alternatives were tried, accurately articulates and supports the reasoning behind the order of their selection, and the extent to which each overcame the obstacles or constraints.

a. Accurately identifies constraints or obstacles.

    4   Accurately and thoroughly describes the relevant constraints or obstacles. Addresses obstacles or constraints that are not immediately apparent.

    3   Accurately identifies the most important constraints or obstacles.

    2   Identifies some constraints or obstacles that are accurate along with some that are not accurate.

    1   Omits the most significant constraints or obstacles.

b. Identifies viable and important alternatives for overcoming the constraints or obstacles.

4   Identifies creative but plausible solutions to the problem under consideration. The solutions address the central difficulties posed by the constraint or obstacle.

3   Proposes alternative solutions that appear plausible and that address the most important constraints or obstacles.

2   Presents alternative solutions for dealing with the obstacles or constraints, but the solutions do not all address the important difficulties.

1   Presents solutions that fail to address critical parts of the problem.

c. Selects and adequately tries out alternatives.

4   Engages in effective, valid, and exhaustive trials of the selected alternatives. Trials go beyond those required to solve the problem and show a commitment to an in-depth understanding of the problem.

3   Puts the selected alternatives to trials adequate to determine their utility.

2   Tries out the alternatives, but the trials are incomplete and important elements are omitted or ignored.

1   Does not satisfactorily test the selected solutions.

d. If other alternatives were tried, accurately articulates and supports the reasoning behind the order of their selection and the extent to which each overcame the obstacles or constraints.

4   Provides a clear, comprehensive summary of the reasoning that led to the selection of secondary solutions. The description includes a review of the decisions that produced the order of selection and how each alternative fared as a solution.

3   Describes the process that led to the ordering of secondary solutions. The description offers a clear, defensible rationale for the ordering of the alternatives and the final selection.

2   Describes the process that led to the ordering of secondary solutions. The description does not provide a clear rationale for the ordering of the alternatives, or the student does not address all the alternatives that were tried.

1   Describes an illogical method for determining the relative value of the alternatives. The student does not present a reasonable review of the strengths and weaknesses of the alternative solutions that were tried and abandoned.

REASONING STRATEGY 12: EXPERIMENTAL INQUIRY

Experimental inquiry involves testing hypotheses that have been generated to explain a phenomenon. It includes four components that can be assessed:

    a. Accurately explains the phenomenon initially observed using appropriate and accepted facts, concepts, or principles.

    b. Makes a logical prediction based on the facts, concepts, or principles underlying the explanation.

    c. Sets up and carries out an activity or experiment that effectively tests the prediction.

    d. Effectively evaluates the outcome of the activity or experiment in terms of the original explanation.

a. Accurately explains the phenomenon initially observed using appropriate and accepted facts, concepts, or principles.

    4   Provides an accurate explanation of the phenomenon. The facts, concepts, or principles used for the explanation are appropriate to the phenomenon and accurately applied. The explanation reflects thorough and careful research or understanding.

    3   Provides an accurate explanation of the phenomenon. The facts, concepts, or principles used in the explanation are appropriate to the phenomenon and accurately applied, with no significant errors.

    2   Explains the phenomenon but misapplies or omits some facts, concepts, or principles that are important for understanding the phenomenon.

    1   Leaves out key facts, concepts, or principles in explaining the phenomenon, or does not use appropriate facts, concepts, or principles to explain the phenomenon.

b. Makes a logical prediction based on the facts, concepts, or principles underlying the explanation.

    4   Makes a verifiable prediction that reflects insight into the character of the phenomenon. The prediction is entirely appropriate to the facts, concepts, or principles used to explain the phenomenon.

    3   Makes a prediction that follows from the facts, concepts, or principles used to explain the phenomenon. The prediction can be verified.

    2   Makes a prediction that reflects a misunderstanding of some aspects of the facts, concepts, or principles used to explain the phenomenon, or makes a prediction that presents difficulties for verification.

    1   Makes a prediction that cannot be verified.

c. Sets up and carries out an activity or experiment that effectively tests the prediction.

4   Sets up and carries out an activity or experiment that is a complete and valid test of the prediction and addresses all important questions raised by the prediction. The activity or experiment is designed to provide complete and accurate data and a model of the experimental design.

3   Sets up and carries out an activity or experiment that is a fair test of the prediction and addresses the most important questions raised by the prediction. The activity or experiment provides accurate data for evaluation.

2   Sets up and carries out an activity or experiment that addresses some important aspects of the prediction, but omits others. The design of the activity or experiment produces some errors in data collection or interpretation.

1   Sets up and carries out an activity or experiment that does not test the central features of the prediction. The experimental design is seriously flawed and the collection of accurate data is unlikely.

d. Effectively evaluates the outcome of the activity or experiment in terms of the original explanation.

4   Provides a complete and accurate explanation of the outcome of the activity or experiment and does so in terms of the relevant facts, concepts, or principles. Provides insights into the nature of the phenomenon studied or the facts, concepts, and principles used to explain it.

3   Provides a complete explanation of the outcome of the activity or experiment with no important errors. Presents the explanation in terms of the relevant facts, concepts, or principles.

2   Provides a general explanation of the outcome of the activity or experiment but omits one or two important aspects, or may not effectively relate the outcome to the facts, concepts, or principles used to generate the prediction.

1   Provides an inaccurate, highly flawed explanation of how the outcome relates to the original explanation.

REASONING STRATEGY 13: INVENTION

Invention involves developing something unique or making unique improvements to a product or process to satisfy an unmet need. It includes four components that can be assessed:

a.   Identifies a process or product to develop or improve to satisfy an unmet need.

b.   Identifies rigorous and important standards or criteria the invention will meet.

c.   Makes detailed and important revisions in the initial process or product.

    d.   Continually revises and polishes the process or product until it reaches a level of completeness consistent with the criteria or standards identified earlier.

a. Identifies a process or product to develop or improve to meet an unmet need.

    4   Proposes a process or product that provides a unique solution to an unmet need. The proposed process or product reflects a high level of creativity.

    3   Proposes a process or product that provides a good answer to the unmet need.

    2   Proposes a process or product that will not adequately satisfy the unmet need.

    1   Proposes a process or product that has little or no relation to the unmet need.

b. Identifies rigorous and important standards or criteria the invention will meet.

    4   Sets out rigorous criteria well suited to the purpose of the invention. The student identifies only the highest achievable standards of quality as acceptable outcomes.

    3   Establishes an appropriate set of criteria for the invention.

    2   Identifies criteria for the invention that may not be completely appropriate for the product or sets standards that do not ensure a worthwhile or completed product.

    1   Establishes criteria that fail to address the most important purposes of the invention. Sets standards so low that little quality can be expected.

c. Makes detailed and important revisions to the initial process or product.

    4   Reviews the process or product at a considerable level of detail. The revisions or improvements clearly bring the process or product closer to fulfilling the purpose for which it is designed. The student's attention to the details of the draft or model makes a high-quality product likely.

    3   Revises the process or product in ways that serve the purpose of the process or product.

    2   Revises the process or product but attempts to address only the most obvious difficulties.

    1   Makes few, if any, attempts at revision and appears satisfied with the initial process or product, although obvious difficulties still remain.

d. Continually revises and polishes the process or product until it reaches a level of completeness consistent with the criteria or standards articulated earlier.

    4   Develops a final process or product that meets the criteria established at a demanding level of quality. The process or product fulfills the purpose for which it was designed. In addition, the process or product reflects creativity and establishes a model for creative work of high quality.

3   Continues revising the process or product until it meets all standards and criteria. The process or product successfully serves the purpose for which it was designed.

2   Revises the process or product until it meets minimum standards.

1   Finishes revising the process or product before it has met minimum standards. The process or product does not meet many important criteria and fails in its purpose.

Rubrics for Information Processing Standards

A.   Effectively interprets and synthesizes information.

4   Interprets the information gathered for a task in accurate and highly insightful ways. Provides a highly creative and unique synthesis of the information.

3   Accurately interprets information gathered for a task and concisely synthesizes it.

2   Makes significant errors in interpreting the information gathered for a task or synthesizes the information imprecisely or awkwardly.

1   Grossly misinterprets the information gathered for the task or fails to synthesize it.

B.   Effectively uses a variety of information-gathering techniques and information resources.

4   Uses the important information-gathering techniques and information resources necessary to complete the task. Identifies little-known information resources or uses unique information-gathering techniques.

3   Uses the important information-gathering techniques and information resources necessary to complete the task.

2   Fails to use some significant information-gathering techniques and information resources necessary to complete the task.

1   Fails to use the most important information-gathering techniques or the major information resources necessary to complete the task.

C.   Accurately assesses the value of information.

4   Analyzes information in detail, accurately and insightfully determining whether it is credible and relevant to a specific task.

3   Accurately determines whether information is credible and relevant to a specific task.

2   Makes some significant errors in determining whether information is credible and relevant to a specific task.

1   Makes little or no attempt to determine whether information is credible and relevant to a specific task or totally misjudges the relevance and credibility of information.

D.   Recognizes where and how projects would benefit from additional information.

4   Insightfully determines the types of information that will benefit a task and effectively seeks out that information.

3   Accurately assesses a task to identify areas requiring additional information for clarification or support and seeks out the needed information.

2   Does not accurately assess the information needs of the task or fails to seek out needed information.

1   Makes little or no attempt to assess whether a task would benefit from additional information.

Rubrics for Effective Communication Standards

A.   Expresses ideas clearly.

4   Clearly and effectively communicates the main idea or theme and provides support that contains rich, vivid, and powerful detail.

3   Clearly communicates the main idea or theme and provides suitable support and detail.

2   Communicates important information but not a clear theme or overall structure.

1   Communicates information as isolated pieces in a random fashion.

B.   Effectively communicates with diverse audiences.

4   Presents information in a style and tone that effectively capitalize on the audience's level of interest and level of knowledge or understanding.

3   Presents information in a style and tone consistent with the audience's level of interest and level of knowledge or understanding.

2   Presents information in a style and tone inappropriate for the audience's level of interest or the audience's level of knowledge.

1   Presents information in a style and tone inappropriate for both the audience's level of interest and level of knowledge.

c.   Effectively communicates in a variety of ways.

4   Uses multiple methods of communication, applying the conventions and rules of those methods in highly creative and imaginative ways.

3   Uses two different methods of communication, applying the conventions and rules of those methods in customary ways.

2   Attempts to use two methods of communication but does not apply the conventions and rules of those methods.

1   Uses only one method of communication when more than one method is clearly needed or requested and does not correctly apply the conventions and rules of that method.

D.   Effectively communicates for a variety of purposes.

4   Clearly communicates a purpose in a highly creative and insightful manner.

3   Uses effective techniques to communicate a clear purpose.

2   Demonstrates an attempt to communicate for a specific purpose but makes significant errors or omissions.

1   Demonstrates no central purpose in the communication or makes no attempt to articulate a purpose.

E.   Creates quality products.

4   Creates a product that exceeds conventional standards.

3   Creates a product that clearly meets conventional standards.

2   Creates a product that does not meet one or a few important standards.

1   Creates a product that does not address the majority of the conventional standards.

Rubrics for Collaboration/Cooperation Standards

A. Works toward the achievement of group goals.

4   Actively helps identify group goals and works hard to meet them.

3   Communicates commitment to the group goals and effectively carries out assigned roles.

2   Communicates a commitment to the group goals but does not carry out assigned roles.

1   Does not work toward group goals or actively works against them.

B. Demonstrates effective interpersonal skills.

4   Actively promotes effective group interaction and the expression of ideas and opinions in a way that is sensitive to the feelings and knowledge base of others.

3   Participates in group interaction without prompting. Expresses ideas and opinions in a way that is sensitive to the feelings and knowledge base of others.

2   Participates in group interaction with prompting or expresses ideas and opinions without considering the feelings and knowledge base of others.

1   Does not participate in group interaction, even with prompting, or expresses ideas and opinions in a way that is insensitive to the feelings or knowledge base of others.

C. Contributes to group maintenance.

4   Actively helps the group identify changes or modifications necessary in the group process and works toward carrying out those changes.

3   Helps identify changes or modifications necessary in the group process and works toward carrying out those changes.

2   When prompted, helps identify changes or modifications necessary in the group process, or is only minimally involved in carrying out those changes.

1   Does not attempt to identify changes or modifications necessary in the group process, even when prompted, or refuses to work toward carrying out those changes.

D.   Effectively performs a variety of roles within a group.

4   Effectively performs multiple roles within the group.

3   Effectively performs two roles within the group.

2   Makes an attempt to perform more than one role within the group but has little success with secondary roles.

1   Rejects opportunities or requests to perform more than one role in the group.

Rubrics for Habits of Mind Standards

A.   Is aware of own thinking.

4   Explains in detail the sequence of thoughts he or she used when facing a task or problem. Provides a detailed analysis of how an awareness of his or her own thinking has enhanced performance.

3   Describes how he or she thought through a task or problem. Provides some ideas about how an awareness of his or her own thinking has enhanced performance.

2   Provides a vague or incomplete description of how he or she thought through a task or problem. Provides only few ideas about how an awareness of his or her own thinking has enhanced performance.

1   Provides a confusing report of the thinking he or she used in completing a task or problem. Cannot describe how performance has been improved.

B.   Makes effective plans.

4   Sets a precise goal. Considers and carries out all necessary subgoals. Creates and adheres to a detailed time line.

3   Sets a goal. Considers and carries out some subgoals. Creates and carries out a useful time line.

2   Begins tasks without a completely defined goal. Makes little attempt to define subgoals or develop a time line.

1   Makes no effort to identify a goal or its related subgoals and time line.

C. Is aware of and uses necessary resources.

4   Performs a careful, detailed assessment of resource needs before beginning a task. Reviews available resources and considers alternatives. Anticipates steps in the process that might require additional demands on resources.

3   Assesses a project to identify areas that require resources. Reviews available and alternative resources to determine whether they are suitable for the project.

2   Considers resource needs as they come up, creating situations in which difficulties that could have been anticipated will stop or hamper a project. Overlooks alternative resources.

1   Does not consider resource needs. Decides to use whatever resources are easily available. Overlooks obvious and necessary resources.

D. Evaluates the effectiveness of own actions.

4   Is sensitive to a wide variety of feedback. Responds promptly when the current approach is clearly not working. Seeks out advice and responses from knowledgeable sources.

3   Is aware of major sources of feedback. Responds and adjusts when correction is needed. Listens to the advice of others.

2   Is insensitive to some important sources of feedback. Rejects some negative feedback. Has difficulty accepting advice.

1   Ignores major sources of feedback. Responds negatively to unfavorable information.

D. Is sensitive to feedback.

4   Reviews actions thoroughly and from as many points of view as is useful. Reviews actions for both immediate and long-term effects. Finds value in lessons learned from both success and failure.

3   Reviews actions from a reasonably objective perspective. Considers short-term effects. Finds lessons in what worked well.

2   Reviews actions from highly subjective perspective. Rarely considers the effects of actions. Gleans few lessons from the task.

1   Makes no effort to review actions.

F. Is accurate and seeks accuracy.

4   Pays close attention to detail when appropriate. Checks against all important sources. Recognizes inaccuracies quickly and makes corrections that not only clear up the identified errors, but add greater clarity to the whole.

3   Pays adequate attention to detail. Checks several sources. Recognizes and corrects major inaccuracies.

2   Tries to be accurate but overlooks important details. Doesn't check enough sources to assure accuracy of important points. Doesn't recognize and correct some important errors.

1   Does not check important details for accuracy. Makes little effort to review for accuracy.

G. Is clear and seeks clarity.

4   The student's entire work is free of confusing parts or elements.

3   The most important elements of the student's work are free of confusion.

2   The student's work has some confusing components that significantly affect the clarity of the whole.

1   The student's entire work is confusing.

H. Is open-minded.

4   Seeks out different and opposing points of view. Considers alternative views impartially and rationally.

3   Is aware of points of view that differ from own. Makes a concerted effort to consider alternative views.

2   Is aware that his or her perspective is not completely shared by all. Pays mild attention to alternative viewpoints.

1   Assumes his or her own perspective is universally accepted. Deliberately avoids other perspectives.

I. Restrains impulsivity.

4   Carefully considers a situation to determine if more study is required before acting. When further study is required, investigates thoroughly before acting.

3   Considers whether more study is required before acting. When further study is required, gathers sufficient information before acting.

2   Cursorily considers whether more study is required before acting. When further study is required, gathers sufficient information before acting.

1   Does not consider whether more study is required before acting.

J. Takes a position when the situation warrants it.

4   Takes a position that is appropriate for the circumstances and introduces a valuable and unrepresented perspective. Provides strong supporting evidence for the position.

3   Takes a position that is appropriate for the circumstances and supports an underrepresented perspective. Provides sufficient justification for the position.

2   Takes a position that the situation does not completely warrant or that is redundant. Does not provide sufficient supporting evidence for the position.

1   Takes a position that is inappropriate for the situation. Presents a position that cannot be supported by evidence.

K. Is sensitive to the feelings and level of knowledge of others.

4   Demonstrates insight concerning the feelings and levels of knowledge of others and exhibits this insight while communicating. Encourages respect for individual differences and sensitivities.

3   Shows the ability to communicate with persons of diverse knowledge and sensitivities. Encourages respect for the feelings, knowledge, and abilities of others.

2   Has difficulty adjusting communications to accommodate persons of diverse knowledge and sensitivities. Does little to encourage respect in others for individual differences.

1   Demonstrates an inability to work or communicate with others of differing knowledge and abilities. Work reflects apathy or callousness towards the feelings of others.

L. Engages intensely in tasks even when answers or solutions are not immediately apparent.

4   Demonstrates strong determination in the pursuit of a solution. Monitors his or her level of involvement and develops and uses a number of strategies to keep self on task.

3   Shows determination in the pursuit of a solution. Uses strategies to keep self on track.

---

2   Makes some effort to resolve a difficult problem but does not spend sufficient time and effort on the problem. Is easily derailed and does not use strategies to keep self on task.

1   Shows evidence of quitting the challenge early, before really trying to solve a problem.

M. Pushes the limits of own knowledge and ability.

4   Seeks out a highly challenging task and works on the task until it is completed or until attaining significant understandings from the task.

3   Accepts the challenge presented and works on the task until it is completed or until attaining significant understandings from the task.

2   Accepts the challenge presented and makes an initial attempt to complete the task, but quits before completing it or attaining significant understandings.

1   Does not accept the challenge.

N. Generates, trusts, and maintains own standards of evaluation.

4   Generates personal standards for completion of the task that significantly raise the quality level of the task. Incorporates those standards into the final product.

3   Generates personal standards for completion of the task and incorporates those standards into the final product.

2   Generates personal standards for the task but does not incorporate them into the final product.

1   Does not generate personal standards for the task.

O. Generates new ways of viewing a situation outside the boundaries of standard convention.

4   Explores as many alternatives as time and resources will allow and analyzes how alternatives will affect the outcome of the task. The alternatives examined illustrate extremely diverse but highly useful ways of looking at the situation.

3   Generates alternative ways of approaching the task and analyzes how the task would be affected by each. Some alternatives show originality in the approach to the task.

2   Considers few alternative ways of viewing the situation; those identified are highly predictable.

1   Remains inflexible. Applies conventional approaches to the situation even when the results are clearly not satisfactory.

7

Summary Rubrics

Summary Rubrics for Content Standards

A. Generic rubric for declarative standards.

4   Demonstrates a thorough understanding of the important concepts or gener-alizations and provides new insights into some aspect of that information.

3   Displays a complete and accurate understanding of the important concepts or generalizations.

2   Displays an incomplete understanding of the important concepts and gener-alizations and has some notable misconceptions.

1   Demonstrates severe misconceptions about the concepts and generalizations.

Note that this generic rubric must be rewritten to include the concepts and generalizations important to the declarative standard, as in the example shown here:

Mathematics Example: Understands the importance of geometry in the modern world.

4   Demonstrates a thorough understanding of the importance of geometry in the modern world and provides new insights into some aspects of geometry's role.

3   Displays a complete and accurate understanding of the importance of geome-try in the modern world.

2   Displays an incomplete understanding of the importance of geometry in the modern world.

1   Demonstrates severe misconceptions about the importance of geometry in the modern world.

B.   Generic rubric for procedural standards.

4   Demonstrates mastery of the important strategies and skills. Can perform them without error and with little or no conscious effort.

3   Carries out the important strategies and skills without significant error and with relative ease.

2   Makes a number of errors when performing important strategies and skills, but can complete a rough approximation of them.

1   Makes many critical errors when performing important strategies and skills.

Note that this generic rubric must be rewritten to include the strategies and skills important to the procedural standards, as in the example shown here:

Mathematics Example: Effectively and efficiently transforms quantities in one system to those in other systems.

4   Demonstrates mastery of the process of transforming quantities in one system to those in other systems.

3   Carries out the processes of transforming quantities in one system to those in other systems without significant errors and with relative ease.

2   Makes a number of errors when transforming quantities in one system to those in other systems but can complete a rough approximation of the processes.

1   Makes many critical errors when transforming quantities in one system to those in other systems.

Summary Rubrics for Complex Thinking Standards

A.   Effectively translates issues and situations into meaningful tasks that have a clear purpose.

4   Consistently translates issues or situations into well-articulated tasks that have clearly defined goals and well-articulated thinking processes. When appropriate, anticipates difficulties and develops plans to overcome them.

3   Consistently translates issues and situations into tasks that have clearly defined goals and identifiable thinking processes.

2   Sporadically translates issues and situations into tasks that have clearly defined goals and identifiable thinking processes.

1   Rarely, if ever, translates issues or situations into tasks that have clearly defined goals and identifiable thinking processes.

B. Effectively uses a variety of complex reasoning strategies.

4   Demonstrates mastery of a variety of complex thinking processes and consistently applies the processes effectively.

3   Demonstrates competency in a number of complex thinking processes and usually applies the processes effectively.

2   Demonstrates ability in a number of complex thinking processes, but does not have a full complement of skills for managing complex issues.

1   Has a severely limited range of complex thinking skills for managing complex tasks.

Summary Rubrics for Information Processing Standards

A. Effectively interprets and synthesizes information.

4   Consistently interprets the information gathered for tasks in accurate and highly insightful way and provides highly creative and unique syntheses of that information.

3   Consistently interprets the information gathered for tasks accurately and synthesizes the information concisely.

2   Sporadically interprets information gathered for tasks accurately and synthesizes the information concisely.

1   Rarely, if ever, interprets information gathered for tasks accurately or synthesizes the information concisely.

B. Effectively uses a variety of information-gathering techniques and information resources.

4   Demonstrates an extensive knowledge of basic information resources and commands a wide range of information-gathering techniques. Demonstrates creativity and resourcefulness in collecting data and creating original data.

3   Demonstrates a knowledge of basic information resources and commands a useful range of information-gathering techniques.

2   Demonstrates a knowledge of some basic information resources but is not aware of all necessary resources, or has command of a limited set of information-gathering techniques.

1 Demonstrates little familiarity with basic information resources or demonstrates a command of only a few basic information-gathering techniques.

C. Accurately assesses the value of information.

4 Consistently analyzes information in detail, accurately and insightfully determining whether it is credible and relevant to tasks.

3 Consistently and accurately determines whether information is credible and relevant to tasks.

2 Sporadically but accurately determines whether information is credible and relevant to tasks.

1 Rarely, if ever, accurately determines whether information is credible and relevant to tasks.

D. Recognizes where and how projects would benefit from additional information.

4 Consistently makes insightful determinations of the types of information that would benefit tasks and effectively seeks out that information.

3 Consistently and accurately assesses tasks to identify areas requiring additional information for clarification or support and seeks out the needed information.

2 Sporadically but accurately assesses tasks to identify areas requiring additional information and seeks out the needed information.

1 Rarely, if ever, accurately assesses tasks to identify areas requiring additional information or seeks out the needed information.

Summary Rubrics for Effective Communication Standards

A. Expresses ideas clearly.

4 Consistently communicates information effectively by providing a clear main idea or theme with support that contains rich, vivid, and powerful detail.

3 Consistently communicates information by providing a clear main idea or theme with sufficient support and detail.

2 Sporadically communicates information by providing a clear main idea or theme with sufficient support and detail.

1   Rarely, if ever, communicates information by providing a clear main idea or theme with sufficient support and detail.

B.   Effectively communicates with diverse audiences.

---

4   Demonstrates an ability to adjust tone and style to a wide and highly diverse range of audiences.

3   Demonstrates the ability to adjust tone and style to different audiences.

2   Demonstrates the ability to communicate with a restricted range of audiences only.

1   Does not demonstrate the ability to adjust tone or style for different audiences.

C.   Effectively communicates in a variety of ways.

---

4   Demonstrates an ability to creatively and effectively use many diverse methods of communication.

3   Demonstrates an ability to effectively use diverse methods of communication.

2   Demonstrates an ability to use only a few methods of communication.

1   Demonstrates an ability to use only one or two methods of communication.

D.   Effectively communicates for a variety of purposes.

---

4   Demonstrates an ability to communicate for a wide and diverse variety of purposes.

3   Demonstrates an ability to communicate for different purposes.

2   Demonstrates an ability to communicate for a restricted range of purposes.

1   Does not demonstrate the ability to change the purpose of communications.

E.   Creates quality products.

---

4   Consistently creates products that exceed conventional standards.

3   Consistently creates products that clearly meet conventional standards.

2   Sporadically creates products that clearly meet conventional standards.

1   Rarely, if ever, creates products that meet conventional standards.

Summary Rubrics for Collaboration/ Cooperation Standards

A. Works toward the achievement of group goals.

4   Consistently and actively helps identify group goals and works hard to meet them.

3   Consistently communicates commitment to group goals and carries out assigned roles.

2   Sporadically communicates commitment to group goals and carries out assigned roles.

1   Rarely, if ever, communicates commitment to group goals or carries out assigned roles.

B. Demonstrates effective interpersonal skills.

4   Consistently and actively helps promote effective group interaction and expresses ideas and opinions in ways that are sensitive to the feelings or knowledge base of others.

3   Consistently participates in group interaction without prompting and expresses ideas and opinions in ways that are sensitive to the feelings and knowledge base of others.

2   Sporadically participates in group interaction without prompting and expresses ideas and opinions in ways that are sensitive to the feelings and knowledge base of others.

1   Rarely, if ever, participates in group interaction without prompting or expresses ideas and opinions in ways that are sensitive to the feelings and knowledge base of others.

C. Contributes to group maintenance.

4   Consistently and actively helps the group identify changes or modifications necessary in group processes and works toward carrying out those changes.

3   Consistently helps identify changes or modifications necessary in group processes and works toward carrying out those changes.

2   Sporadically helps identify changes or modifications necessary in group processes and sometimes works toward carrying out those changes.

---

1   Rarely, if ever, helps identify changes or modifications necessary in group processes and seldom works toward carrying out those changes.

D.   Effectively performs a variety of roles within a group.

4   Demonstrates an ability to perform a wide range of roles within a group.

3   Demonstrates an ability to perform different roles within a group.

2   Demonstrates an ability to perform a restricted range of roles within a group.

1   Does not demonstrate an ability to change roles within a group.

Summary Rubrics for Habits of Mind Standards

A.   Is aware of own thinking.

4   Consistently and accurately explains in detail the sequence of thoughts he or she uses when faced with a task or problem, and provides analyses of how an awareness of own thinking has enhanced his or her performance.

3   Consistently and accurately describes how he or she thinks through tasks or problems and how an awareness of own thinking enhances his or her performance.

2   Sporadically but accurately describes how he or she thinks through tasks or problems and how an awareness of own thinking enhances his or her performance.

1   Rarely, if ever, accurately describes how he or she thinks through tasks or problems or how an awareness of his or her thinking enhances performance.

B.   Makes effective plans.

4   Consistently sets precise goals, considers and carries out all necessary subgoals, and creates and adheres to detailed time lines.

3   Consistently sets goals, carries out some subgoals, and creates and carries out useful time lines.

2   Sporadically sets goals, carries out some subgoals, and creates and carries out useful time lines.

1   Rarely, if ever, sets goals, carries out subgoals, or creates and carries out useful time lines.

C. Is aware of and uses necessary resources.

4   Consistently performs careful, detailed assessments of resource needs before beginning tasks. Reviews available resources and considers alternatives. Anticipates steps in tasks that might require additional demands on resources.

3   Consistently assesses projects to identify areas that require resources. Reviews available and alternative resources to determine whether they are suitable for the projects.

2   Sporadically assesses projects to identify resources needed for tasks, and often overlooks alternative resources.

1   Rarely, if ever, assesses projects to identify resources needed, and often overlooks obvious and necessary resources.

D. Is sensitive to feedback.

4   Is consistently sensitive to a wide variety of feedback. Always responds promptly when the current approach to the task is clearly not working and seeks out advice and responses from knowledgeable sources.

3   Is consistently aware of major sources of feedback and invariably responds and makes adjustments when corrections are needed. Listens to the advice of others.

2   Is sometimes aware of major sources of feedback. Sporadically responds and makes adjustments when corrections are needed. Sometimes listens to the advice of others.

1   Rarely, if ever, is aware of major sources of feedback. Seldom responds and makes adjustments when corrections are needed. Doesn't listen to the advice of others.

E. Evaluating the effectiveness of own actions.

4   Consistently reviews actions thoroughly and from as many points of view as is useful, evaluates actions for both immediate and long-term impact, and finds value in lessons learned from both success and failure.

3   Consistently reviews actions from a reasonably objective perspective, considers short-term effects, and finds lessons in what works well.

2   Sporadically reviews actions from a reasonably objective perspective, considers short-term effects, and finds lessons in what works well.

1   Rarely, if ever, reviews actions from a reasonably objective perspective, considers short-term effects, or finds lessons in what works well.

F. Is accurate and seeks accuracy.

4   Consistently pays close attention to detail when appropriate, checks information against all important sources, recognizes inaccuracies quickly, and makes corrections that not only clear up the identified errors, but add greater clarity to the whole.

3   Consistently pays adequate attention to detail, checks several sources, and recognizes and corrects major inaccuracies.

2   Sporadically pays adequate attention to detail, checks several sources, and recognizes and corrects major inaccuracies.

1   Rarely, if ever, pays adequate attention to detail, checks several sources, or recognizes and corrects major inaccuracies.

G. Is clear and seeks clarity.

4   Consistently creates works that are completely free of confusing elements.

3   Consistently creates works whose key elements are free of confusion.

2   Sporadically creates works whose key elements are free of confusion.

1   Rarely, if ever, creates works whose key elements are free of confusion.

H. Is open-minded.

4   Consistently seeks out different and opposing points of view and considers alternative views impartially and rationally.

3   Is consistently aware of points of view that differ from his or her own and always makes a concerted effort to consider alternative views.

2   Is at times aware of points of view that differ from his or her own and sporadically makes an effort to consider alternative views.

1   Rarely, if ever, is aware of points of view that differ from his or her own and seldom makes an effort to consider alternative views.

I. Restrains impulsivity.

4   Consistently and carefully considers situations to determine if more study is required before acting; when further study is required, engages in detailed investigation before acting.

3   Consistently considers situations to determine whether more study is required before acting; when further study is required, gathers sufficient information before acting.

2   Sporadically considers situations to determine whether more study is required before acting; when further study is required, sometimes gathers sufficient information before acting.

1   Rarely, if ever, considers situations to determine whether more study is required before acting; when further study is required, usually doesn't gathers sufficient information before acting.

J.   Takes a position when the situation warrants it.

4   Consistently takes positions that are appropriate to the circumstances and introduce valuable and unrepresented perspectives. Always provides strong supporting evidence for the positions.

3   Consistently takes a position that is appropriate for the circumstances and supports an underrepresented perspective; always provides sufficient justifications for the positions.

2   Sporadically takes a position that is appropriate to the circumstances and supports an the identified position; sometimes provides sufficient justifications for the positions.

1   Rarely, if ever, takes a position that is appropriate to the situation and supports an underrepresented position; seldom provides sufficient justifications for the positions.

K.   Is sensitive to the feelings and level of knowledge of others.

4   Consistently demonstrates insight concerning the feelings and levels of knowledge of others and exhibits this insight while communicating. Always encourages respect for individual differences and sensitivities.

3   Consistently shows the ability to communicate with persons of diverse knowledge and sensitivities and encourages respect for the feelings, knowledge, and abilities of others.

2   Sporadically shows the ability to communicate with persons of diverse knowledge and sensitivities and encourages respect for the feelings, knowledge, and abilities of others.

1   Rarely, if ever, shows the ability to communicate with persons of diverse knowledge and sensitivities or encourages respect for the feelings, knowledge, and abilities of others.

L. Engages intensely in tasks even when answers or solutions are not immediately apparent.

4   Consistently demonstrates strong determination in the pursuit of solutions, monitors his or her level of involvement, and develops and uses a number of strategies to keep self on task.

3   Consistently shows determination in the pursuit of solutions and uses strategies to keep self on track.

2   Sporadically shows determination in the pursuit of solutions and uses strategies to keep self on track.

1   Rarely, if ever, shows determination in the pursuit of solutions or uses strategies to keep self on track.

M. Pushing the limits of own knowledge and ability.

4   Consistently seeks out highly challenging tasks and works on the tasks until they are completed or until attaining significant understandings.

3   Consistently accepts the challenges presented and works on tasks until they are completed or until attaining significant understandings.

2   Sporadically accepts the challenges presented and works on tasks until they are completed or until attaining significant understandings.

1   Rarely, if ever, accepts the challenges presented and seldom works on tasks until they are completed or until attaining significant understandings.

N. Generates, trusts, and maintains own standards of evaluation.

4   Consistently generates personal standards for tasks that significantly raise the quality level of those tasks and incorporates the standards into the final products.

3   Consistently generates personal standards for tasks and incorporates those standards into the final products.

2   Sporadically generates personal standards for tasks and incorporates those standards into the final products.

1   Rarely, if ever, generates personal standards for tasks or incorporates them into the final products.

O. **Generates new ways of viewing a situation outside the boundaries of standard conventions.**

4   Consistently explores as many alternatives as time and resources will allow and analyzes how the identified alternatives will affect outcomes. The alternatives illustrate extremely diverse but highly useful ways of looking at situations.

3   Consistently generates alternative ways of approaching tasks and analyzes how the alternatives will affect those tasks. Some alternatives show originality in the approach to the tasks.

2   Sporadically generates alternative ways of approaching tasks and analyzes how the alternatives will affect those tasks. Some alternatives show originality in the approach to the tasks.

1   Rarely, if ever, generates alternative ways of approaching tasks or analyzes how the alternatives will affect those tasks. Few alternatives show originality in the approach to tasks.

8

Rubrics for Students

Complex Thinking Standards

A. **I analyze information and situations by turning them into projects that help me think about them in specific ways.**

4   I analyze information or a situation by turning it into a detailed project that will make me think about it in new ways. I explain exactly what kind of thinking I will have to do to complete the project and what I will learn as a result of doing it. I even predict what parts will be difficult for me.

3   I analyze information or a situation by turning it into a project that will make me think about it; I explain what kind of thinking the project will require me to do and what it will look like when it is complete.

2   I analyze information or a situation and turn it into a project, but parts of the description are not clear and the purpose of the project is confusing.

1   I try to analyze information or a situation, but I do not make clear what the project is. I also do not have a clear purpose for the project.

B. **I use a variety of complex reasoning processes well.**

REASONING STRATEGY 1: COMPARISON

   a. **I select useful and important items to compare.**

4   I select items that are useful and important and help me make interesting comparisons; I select items that might be different from what other people select because I want to see things in new ways as a result of doing this comparison.

3   I select items that are useful and important and help me achieve the goal for the comparison.

2   I select items that will allow me to do a comparison, but the items may not be very useful or important and may even cause some problems as I do the comparison.

1   I select items that are not useful or important or that do not work for the comparison.

b. I select useful and important characteristics on which to compare the selected items.

4   I select characteristics that focus on the most useful and important information about the items being compared. The characteristics will help me see the items in new and unusual ways.

3   I select characteristics that are useful and important and will help me think about items in interesting ways.

2   I select some characteristics that will help me do some comparing of items, but a few of the characteristics are not very useful in the comparison.

1   I select unimportant characteristics that are not at all useful in the comparison; or I select items that I cannot even compare.

c. I accurately describe how the items are the same and different for each characteristic.

4   I accurately describe the important ways the items are the same and different for each of the characteristics; I also explain interesting ideas and conclusions that occur to me as a result of the comparison.

3   I accurately describe important ways the items are the same and different for each of the characteristics.

2   I make some errors when I describe how the items are the same and different for each of the characteristics.

1   I make many significant errors when I try to describe how the items are the same and different for each of the characteristics.

REASONING STRATEGY 2: CLASSIFICATION

a. I select important items to classify.

4   I select important and interesting items to classify; they may even be difficult to classify and may force me to think about things in new ways.

3   I select items that are important and make me think when I classify them.

2   I select items that are not very important or that will be simple to quickly put in categories.

1   I select items that are unimportant or have nothing to do with the reason I am doing the classification.

b. I create useful categories for classifying the items.

4   I create categories that make me think about the items in interesting and different ways.

3   I create categories that make me think about important characteristics of the items.

2   I create categories that allow me to classify but don't really make me think about the important characteristics of the items.

1   I create categories that use only unimportant characteristics of the items.

c. I describe accurate and complete rules for deciding which items go in each category.

4   I clearly and completely describe the rules for deciding which items go in each category; I describe these rules in a way that forces me to think about the items in interesting and unusual ways.

3   I clearly describe rules for deciding which items go in each category, wording my descriptions in ways that eliminate any confusion about where to place the items.

2   I describe the rules for deciding which items go in each category, but I leave things out and create confusion, or I include information about the categories that does not really help put the items in correct categories.

1   I list rules, but they do not describe the categories.

d. I accurately place the items in the categories.

4   I place each item in the correct category and describe why it fits in that category; I also describe interesting ideas and thoughts that occur to me while I am doing this.

3   I place each item in the correct category and, when I need to, I describe why it fits in the category.

2   I make some mistakes when I place items in categories and, even when it would be helpful, I don't describe why an item fits in a category.

1   I make many errors when placing items in categories and do not describe why I placed them in specific categories.

REASONING STRATEGY 3: INDUCTION

a. I select and describe specific pieces of information to use in making general conclusions or statements.

4   I clearly and accurately select and describe all important pieces of information to use in making and supporting general conclusions or statements; I am careful and think in new and interesting ways when I select and use the specific pieces of information.

3   I accurately select and describe all important pieces of information to use in making and supporting general conclusions or statements.

2   I select some specific pieces of information that are not really important in making and supporting general conclusions or statements or I miss important pieces of information related to the conclusions or statements.

1   I select unimportant pieces of information.

b. I think about the information and explain interesting ideas or meanings I find in it.

4   I explain interesting ideas or meanings I find in the information; the ideas or meanings I find show that I have thought a lot about the information and used all my knowledge to find these interesting ideas or meanings.

3   I explain interesting ideas or meanings I find in the information; the ideas or meanings are generally accurate and important.

2   I explain ideas or meanings I find in the information, but some of them are inaccurate because I did not really understand the information.

1   I explain ideas or meanings I find in the information, but they are inaccurate, don't make sense, or do not really relate to the information.

c. I make general conclusions from the specific pieces of information or observations.

4   I make clear, general conclusions from the specific pieces of information or observations; the conclusions make sense and show that I understand how to think about and combine specific information and observations to come to interesting general conclusions.

3   I make general conclusions from the specific pieces of information or observations; the conclusions generally show I have used the information or observations in a way that makes sense.

2   I make conclusions from the specific pieces of information or observations and describe how I used the information, but some conclusions and descriptions don't make sense.

1   I make conclusions that don't make sense, and I can't really describe how I used the information and observations.

REASONING STRATEGY 4: DEDUCTION

a. I select an important and useful general statement in information I am analyzing.

4   I select an important general statement in the information that adds to the understanding of the information in a way that goes beyond the obvious meanings others see.

3   I select an important general statement that helps to explain the information I am analyzing.

2   I select an important general statement that is related to the information I am analyzing, but does not really help to explain it.

1   I select a general statement, but it is not related to the information or adds nothing to the understanding of the information.

b. I accurately explain the meaning of the general statement.

4   I accurately and clearly explain the meaning of the general statement and show how it can be used in ways that may not be obvious to others.

3   I accurately and clearly explain the meaning of the general statement.

2   I explain the meaning of the general statement, but make some errors.

1   I explain the meaning of the general statement, but make major errors.

c. I accurately explain how the general statement applies to other information.

4   I accurately explain how the general statement applies to other information. I find ways to accurately apply it that other people generally miss and show how applying it in these new ways will add to the understanding of the entire subject that is being analyzed.

3   I explain, with minor errors, how the general statement applies to other information; the explanation provides a useful way of thinking about the subject that is being analyzed.

2   I explain some important ways of applying the statement to other information, but I make some errors or include ways of applying the information that are not useful.

1   I explain some ways of applying the statement, but they do not make sense or do not relate to the subject.

REASONING STRATEGY 5: ERROR ANALYSIS

a. I find and describe major errors in information I read or hear, or when watching someone do something.

4   I accurately find and describe all errors in the information or process I am analyzing; I clearly describe each one and tell why it is clearly an error; I even find minor errors that many people miss.

3   I accurately find and describe all important errors in the information or process I am analyzing; I describe each and tell why it is an error.

2   I miss some important errors when I am analyzing information or a process, or sometimes I describe errors and find out they are not really errors.

1   I don't find important errors or I frequently describe errors that I find out are not really errors.

b. I accurately describe how the errors affect the information or process I am analyzing.

4   I accurately and completely describe how the errors affect or cause problems in the information or process; I explain the major effects or problems that are easy to see, but I also explain little things that could happen because of the error.

3   I accurately describe, with some details, how the errors affect or cause problems in the information or process.

2   I describe how the errors affect or cause problems in the information or process but I leave out some important effects or problems, or my description is not entirely accurate.

1   I do not accurately describe the effects or problems the errors cause in the information or process, or I describe effects or problems that do not really exist.

c. I accurately describe how to correct the errors.

4   I describe workable and creative ways of correcting the errors so all possible effects or problems will be taken care of; my ideas for correcting the errors show that I have used my knowledge about the information and process and have thought about more than one workable way of correcting the errors.

3   I describe workable ways of correcting the errors; my ideas take care of the major effects or problems the errors cause.

2   I describe some ways of correcting the errors but I my ideas sometimes do not take care of the effects or problems the errors cause.

1   My ideas for correcting the errors are not workable or would not take care of the effects or problems the errors cause.

REASONING STRATEGY 6: CONSTRUCTING SUPPORT

a.   I accurately make a statement that needs to be supported with more information.

4   I accurately and clearly make a statement that needs to be supported with more information; this statement may have been mistaken by others as a fact, but I recognize that it needs support.

3   I accurately make a clear statement that needs to be supported with more information.

2   I make a statement that needs to be supported with more information, but sometimes I add too much to the statement and confuse it with other types of information.

1   I make a statement that needs no support.

b.   I provide enough information to support the statement.

4   I clearly and accurately present all the available information that strongly supports the statement. I describe how important each piece of information is to the support of the statement. I also explain what information is not available and what problems the missing information might cause.

3   I clearly and accurately present all the important information that strongly supports the statement.

2   I present some important information that supports the statement, but I don't provide enough information or I leave out necessary information.

1   I don't present information that supports the statement.

c.   I explain situations where the statement does not apply.

4   I accurately explain situations where the statement does not apply. My explanation shows that I have carefully thought about the statement and understand where it does and does not apply. It also helps support the statement and provides a way of understanding the statement from a different point of view.

3   I accurately explain situations where the statement does not apply. My explanation helps support the statement.

2   I explain some situations where the statement does not apply, but I leave out important points or do not explain them accurately.

1   I don't explain situations where the statement does not apply.

REASONING STRATEGY 7: ABSTRACTING

a. **I select a significant situation or meaningful information that has within it an identifiable pattern. I identify that pattern and then compare it with the relationships or patterns in another situation or in other information.**

  4 I select a significant situation or meaningful information that has within it an interesting general pattern that could be compared to a pattern in other situations or in other information; the information or situation I select is not something others typically would choose, but I explain how I see it in a different way and why I think it would be a good topic for abstracting.

  3 I select a significant situation or meaningful information that has within it a general pattern that could be compared to patterns in other situations or in other information.

  2 I select information or a situation that has a general pattern that could be compared to other information or situations, but the information or situation I select is not really very useful or important.

  1 I select information or a situation that is not very important or useful. It also does not really have a general pattern that could be compared to other specific information or situations.

b. **I find a general pattern in the specific situation or information.**

  4 I find a general pattern that includes the important parts of the situation or information and also helps show the interesting ideas and meanings in the situation or information. The general relationship or pattern will clearly help me compare patterns in other specific situations or information.

  3 I find a general pattern in the specific situation or information that is accurate, includes the important ideas, and could be used to compare patterns in other specific situations or information.

  2 I find a general pattern in the specific situation or information that includes some important ideas, but it is not completely accurate or it leaves out some important parts of the situation or information.

  1 I don't find a general pattern that is accurate and includes important ideas.

c. **I accurately explain how the general pattern in the specific situation or information is the same as the general pattern in another situation or set of information.**

  4 I select another situation or set of information and describe how it has a pattern that is the same as the pattern in the first situation or set of information. The second situation or set of information is interesting and isn't what most people would typically select. My comparison of the two situations or sets of information brings out many ideas that help show new and interesting ways of looking at both situations or sets of information.

3   I select a second situation or set of information and describe how it has a pattern that is the same as the pattern in my first situation or set of information. The second situation or set of information is important, and my comparison of the two is useful and interesting.

2   I select a second situation or set of information that is only a little bit similar to the first situation or set of information. The two situations or sets of information don't really have matching patterns.

1   I select a second situation or set of information that is not at all similar to the first situation or set of information.

REASONING STRATEGY 8: ANALYZING PERSPECTIVES

a.   I find and describe a topic on which people disagree and explain the areas of disagreement

4   I find and accurately describe a topic on which people disagree. I explain the obvious and specific areas of disagreement, but I also find and explain less obvious causes of disagreement.

3   I find and accurately describe a topic on which people disagree and explain the areas of disagreement.

2   I find a topic on which people disagree, but I make errors in explaining the specific areas of disagreement.

1   I find a topic on which people disagree, but I do not find or describe any specific areas of disagreement.

b.   I state an opinion on the topic and explain the reasons for that opinion.

4   I clearly state an opinion on the topic and explain the reasons for that opinion. I also describe the thinking that might lead to the opinion, and I explain the strengths, weaknesses, and errors in that thinking.

3   I clearly state an opinion on the topic and explain some of the important reasons for that opinion. I do not explain the thinking that might lead to the opinion.

2   I clearly state an opinion on the topic, but I do not clearly explain the reasons for that opinion.

1   I do not state a clear opinion.

c. **I state an opinion different from the first one and explain the reasons for that opinion.**

4   I clearly state a detailed opinion different from the first one and explain the important reasons for that opinion. I describe the thinking that might lead to that opinion, and I explain the strengths, weaknesses, and errors in that thinking.

3   I clearly state an opinion different from the first one and explain the important reasons a person might have for that opinion. I do not describe the thinking that would lead someone to that opinion.

2   I clearly state an opinion different from the first one, but I do not clearly explain the reasons for that opinion.

1   I do not state a clear opinion different from the first one.

REASONING STRATEGY 9: DECISION MAKING

a. **I identify important and useful choices for my decision-making task.**

4   I identify all the important and useful choices for my decision-making task and describe them with details.

3   I identify and describe the most important and useful choices for my decision-making task.

2   I identify some choices that are important and useful to the decision-making task, but I also identify some that are not very important or useful.

1   I identify choices that are not at all important or useful for the decision-making task.

b. **I identify important criteria to use when I evaluate my choices.**

4   I identify and describe important criteria to use when I evaluate my choices. My criteria show that I have thought about and understand the decision and have carefully considered each criterion before selecting it.

3   I identify and describe important criteria to use when I evaluate my choices.

2   I identify some important criteria to use when I evaluate my choices, but I also identify some criteria that are not very important or I leave out some very important criteria.

1   I identify criteria that are unimportant or unrelated to the decision-making task.

c. I accurately describe how each choice relates to each criterion.

4   I accurately describe, with details, how each choice relates to each criterion. For some of the criteria, I even compare the choices to clearly show the differences among the choices.

3   I accurately describe how each choice relates to each criterion.

2   I do not describe how each choice relates to each criterion or I make some mistakes when I relate the choices to the criteria.

1   I do not describe how the choices relate to the criteria or I make many errors when I describe how the choices relate to the criteria.

d. I select the choice that meets my criteria and answers the question that created the need for a decision.

4   I select a choice after carefully considering how the choices match the criteria. I can explain why my choice effectively answers the question that originally created the need for a decision. I also explain any important and interesting ideas that occurred to me or other things I learned during the process of making this decision.

3   I select the choice that best matches my criteria. The choice provides a satisfactory answer to the question that originally created the need for a decision.

2   I select a choice that matches some criteria, but it may not be the best choice because I ignored or did not see a better match.

1   I select a choice without giving much thought to how it matches the criteria, or I cannot explain how my choice matches the criteria.

REASONING STRATEGY 10: INVESTIGATION (DEFINITIONAL, HISTORICAL, AND PROJECTIVE)

a. I find and explain the information that everyone agrees is clear or is known about the concept I am defining (definitional investigation), the past event I am describing (historical investigation), or the future event I am predicting (projective investigation).

4   I find and accurately describe as much as possible about what is already clear or known about the topic. I check my information carefully to make sure it is correct. I even find information that very few people know and show why it is important to my topic.

3   I find and accurately describe the important information that is already clear or known about the topic I am investigating.

2   I find some important information that is already clear or known about the topic, but I miss important information or inaccurately describe my topic.

1   I find little or no information that is already clear or known about the topic.

b. I find and explain the things about the concept I am defining (definitional investigation), the past event I am describing (historical investigation), or the future event I am predicting (projective investigation) that cause people to be confused, unsure, or in disagreement.

4   I find and explain, with details, all the important things about the topic that cause people to be confused, unsure, or in disagreement. I even find things that other people often do not see.

3   I find and explain the most important things about the topic that cause people to be confused, unsure, or in disagreement.

2   I find and explain some of the things about the topic that cause people to be confused, unsure, or in disagreement, but I leave out some important ideas.

1   I do not find any important things about the topic that cause people to be confused, unsure, or in disagreement.

c. I suggest and defend a way of clearing up or settling the things that cause people to be confused, unsure, or in disagreement.

4   I suggest and defend a detailed explanation of the topic that clears up or settles the things that cause people to be confused, unsure, or in disagreement. My explanation makes sense and shows that I understand the problem and have thought about it carefully; it even gives people a new way of looking at the topic.

3   I suggest and defend an explanation of the topic that clears up or settles the things that cause people to be confused, unsure, or in disagreement. My explanation uses information accurately and makes sense.

2   I suggest an explanation of the topic that tries to clear up or settle the things that cause people to be confused, unsure, or in disagreement, but I do not defend it very well or I use some inaccurate information.

1   I suggest an explanation of the topic that does not clear up or settle things, that I cannot defend, or that does not make sense.

REASONING STRATEGY 11: PROBLEM SOLVING

a.   I accurately recognize and describe the limits or barriers that make it difficult for me to achieve my goal.

4   I accurately recognize all the important limits or barriers that make it difficult for me to achieve my goal. I describe, with details, how they make it difficult. I even recognize and describe lesser limits or barriers that make it more difficult to achieve my goal.

3   I accurately recognize and describe the major limits or barriers that make it difficult for me to achieve my goal.

2   I recognize and describe some of the major limits or barriers that make it difficult for me to achieve my goal, but I miss some important ones or inaccurately describe them.

1   I describe what I see as limits or barriers but do not recognize or describe any of the major limits or barriers that make it difficult for me to achieve my goal.

b. I suggest workable and effective solutions for dealing with the limits or barriers so I can achieve my goal.

4   I suggest a number of interesting and workable solutions for dealing with the limits or barriers so I can achieve my goal. My suggestions show I have thought carefully because some of my ideas are very different from what others might suggest; the solutions relate directly to all of the specific problems caused by the limits or barriers.

3   I suggest a number of workable solutions for dealing with the limits or barriers so I can achieve my goal. My suggestions will help me deal with the problems created by the limits or barriers.

2   I suggest several solutions for dealing with the limits or barriers, but some of them do not help solve the important problems created by the limits or barriers.

1   I suggest solutions for dealing with the limits or barriers, but my suggestions do not relate to the problems created by the limits or barriers.

c. I select and try out the best solution.

4   I decide which of my ideas is probably going to be the best solution and set up a way of trying it out to see if it works. I use a method of testing the solution that I know will give me a complete idea of how well it helps me deal with all of the problems created by the specific limits or barriers. I also see if the solution has other unexpected effects that help me achieve my original goal.

3   I select what seems to be the best solution and try it out in a way that will tell me if it works. The test I use helps me decide if the solution is a good one for dealing with the limits or barriers in my problem.

2   I select what seems to be the best solution and try it out, but the way I set up the test does not really tell me how well it works. I still won't know if the solution is a good one for dealing with the limits or barriers.

1   I select what seems to be the best solution, but I do not try it out in a situation that gives me any usable information about how well it works.

d. When I try other solutions besides my first choice, I explain the reasons they were not my first choice and describe how well each of them helps me deal with the limits or barriers in my problem.

4   I explain clearly and with details why I am testing other solutions besides my first choice. I describe the criteria I used to put the solutions in order of importance and tell how the solutions meet the criteria. I then explain how well each solution worked to help me deal with the limits or barriers in my problem.

3   I explain the process I used to put my other solutions in order of importance. The process is clear and makes sense. I also describe how well the solutions helped me deal with the limits or barriers in my problem.

2   I explain the process I used to put my other solutions in order, but the process is not very clear or has some errors; or I do not describe how each of the solutions worked.

1   I explain the process I used to put my other solutions in order, but it makes no sense. I do not describe how well any of the solutions worked.

REASONING STRATEGY 12: EXPERIMENTAL INQUIRY

a. I use accurate and important information to suggest an explanation for something I am studying.

4   I suggest a clear explanation for something I am studying. My explanation includes accurate and important information from a variety of sources. I check my information carefully to make sure it clearly explains what I observe.

3   I suggest a clear explanation for something I am studying. My explanation includes accurate and important information.

2   I suggest an explanation something I am studying. I include some inaccurate information or leave out important information that would have made the explanation clearer.

1   I suggest an explanation for something I am studying, but I include inaccurate or unimportant information and leave out important information.

b. I make a prediction about what would happen if my explanation is correct.

4   I make a prediction about what would happen if my explanation is correct. The prediction can be tested and is based on the information in my explanation. I even add more information to show that I am increasing my knowledge of what I am studying.

3   I make a prediction about what would happen if my explanation is correct. The prediction is based on the information in my explanation and can be tested.

2   I make a prediction about what would happen if my explanation is correct, but the prediction is based on the incorrect use of information in my explanation or is a prediction that would be difficult to test.

1   I make a prediction that cannot be tested.

c. I set up and carry out an experiment (or activity) to find out whether my prediction is accurate.

4   I set up and carry out an experiment that tests all aspects of my prediction. The experiment also produces other useful information and gives answers to other questions related to my prediction. I carefully plan every step of the activity or experiment so that the results are accurate, clear, and usable.

3   I set up and carry out an experiment that does a good job of testing the prediction. I get some accurate, clear, and usable results.

2   I set up and carry out an experiment that tests some parts of my prediction but does not give me complete information. Some of the results are difficult to use in finding out whether my prediction is accurate.

1   I set up and carry out an experiment, but it does not test the prediction. The set-up of the experiment is sloppy and my results are inaccurate or not usable.

d. I accurately evaluate the results of the experiment (or activity) and decide whether my original explanation of what I am studying is correct.

4   I accurately evaluate all the results of the experiment to decide whether my prediction was accurate and the results support my original explanation of what I am studying. I discuss how accurately I used the important information in my original explanation. I also describe what I learn or understand better as a result of doing this experiment.

3   I accurately evaluate the important results of the experiment to decide whether my prediction was accurate. I explain how well the results support my original explanation.

2   I describe some important results of the experiment, but I leave out some important results or have trouble explaining how the results relate to my original explanation.

1   I describe some results, but I make many errors and do not relate the results to my original explanation.

REASONING STRATEGY 13: INVENTION

a. I suggest a process that could be improved upon or a product that could be created.

4   I suggest a process or product that could be improved upon or created. My idea is unusual and extremely useful. It shows that I have studied and thought carefully about what it takes to come up with an idea that will improve people's lives by meeting a specific need.

3   I suggest a process or product that could be improved upon or created. My idea is new and useful.

2   I suggest a process or product that is somewhat useful, but will not really help meet a specific need.

1   I suggest a process or product that is not related to a specific need.

b. I set clear and important standards that my invention will meet.

4   I set clear and useful standards that my invention must meet. I make sure the standards are high enough so that my invention will be the best.

3   I set clear and useful standards that will be my guide to quality as I work on my invention.

2   I set clear standards, but some of them are not very useful for this type of invention or are not high enough to help me do quality work.

1   I set standards that do not really relate to my invention or are so low that it looks like I do not plan to do quality work.

c. As I work on my invention, I make detailed and important changes when necessary.

4   As I work, I study my invention carefully to identify small changes that might make it better. I always go back and think about the need my invention is supposed to meet, and my changes definitely help it better meet that need. My goal is to keep making changes until my invention is the best it can be.

3   As I work, I make important changes when necessary so the invention will meet the need that it is supposed to meet.

2   As I work, I make changes, but only when absolutely necessary.

1   As I work, I make almost no changes. I stick with my first try, even if it does not work very well.

d. I work on my invention until it is complete and has met the standards that I set.

4   I work on my invention until it completely meets or exceeds the standards that I set. The final process or product serves its intended purpose and even goes beyond what I had originally planned.

3   I work on my invention until it meets all the standards that I set. The final product or process serves its intended purpose.

2   I work on my invention only until it barely meets some of the standards I set. It partially serves its intended purpose.

1   I quit work on my invention before it meets the standards I set. The invention does not serve its intended purpose.

Information Processing Standards

A.   I find meaning in information and then combine and organize information to make it useful for my task.

4   I find useful and accurate meaning in information I gather for my task. I understand meanings in information that other people do not see. I then combine and organize information in my own way to express certain ideas.

3   I find useful and accurate meaning in the information I gather for my task, and I combine and organize the information so that it makes sense.

2   I make errors when I look for meaning in information that I gather for my task, and I combine the information inaccurately or in a way that makes it confusing.

1   I make major errors when I look for meaning in information that I gather for my task, and I do not combine or organize information.

B.   I use a variety of methods and resources when gathering information for my task.

4   I use important information resources and useful methods when I gather information for my task. I even find resources that other people don't think of or don't know about. My methods are unusual but effective.

3   I use important information resources and useful methods when I gather information for my task.

2   I miss some important information resources and fail to use some of the best methods when I gather information for my task.

1   I do not use important information resources or the best methods when I gather information for my task.

C. **I accurately determine how valuable specific information may be to my task.**

4   I accurately determine how valuable specific information may be to my task, explaining in detail how and why the information would be useful and whether it is believable. My explanation shows that I understand well the kind of information needed for my task.

3   I accurately determine how valuable specific information may be in my task. I explain how it would be useful and whether it is believable.

2   I make some errors when I determine how valuable specific information may be to my task and explain how useful and believable it is.

1   I do not determine how valuable specific information may be to my task, or I make many major errors when I explain how the information may be useful or whether it is believable.

D. **I recognize when more information is needed and explain how the new information would improve the completed project.**

4   I recognize when more information is needed, even when other people may think the project is fine. I explain how the completed project would benefit from additional information and I describe exactly what information is needed. I then find the information.

3   I recognize that more information would make the completed project better and explain how additional information would improve it. I then find the information.

2   I do not recognize when a project needs more information. Even if I decide more is needed, I do not find the needed information.

1   I do not try to recognize when a project needs more information.

Effective Communication Standards

A. **I communicate ideas clearly.**

4   I communicate ideas by making sure I have a strong main idea or topic and carefully organized details that explain or support the idea or topic. I make sure the details help make the bigger ideas useful and interesting.

3   I communicate ideas by making sure I have a clear main idea or topic and enough details to explain or support the idea or topic.

2   I communicate some important information, but I do not organize it well around a main idea or topic.

1   I communicate information in unorganized pieces.

B.   I communicate well with different audiences.

4   I present information to various audiences in a way that makes the most of their specific knowledge and interests.

3   I present information to various audiences in a way that suits their specific knowledge and interests.

2   I present information to various audiences in a way that does not completely suit their knowledge and interests.

1   I present information to various audiences in a way that conflicts with their knowledge and interests.

C.   I communicate well using a variety of media.

4   I use many methods of communication and I follow the correct processes and use the accepted standards of those mediums. I also use the mediums in new and different ways.

3   I communicate using two mediums and follow the correct process and use the accepted standards for both of those mediums.

2   I try to communicate using two mediums, but I make errors in the processes and misunderstand the accepted standards of the mediums I am using.

1   I do not even try to communicate in more than one medium.

D.   I communicate well for different purposes.

4   I clearly explain the purpose of my communication by selecting and using very effective and original methods. My explanation goes beyond just stating the purpose; it adds meaning to the information I am communicating.

3   I clearly explain the purpose of my communication by selecting and using effective methods.

2   I try to explain the purpose of my communication, but I make errors in the explanation or leave out information that would make it clear.

1   I do not try to explain the purpose of my communication or I don't really have a clear purpose.

Collaboration/Cooperation Standards

A. I work to help achieve the goals of the group.

4   I participate actively and even help lead the group in setting goals. I do the jobs assigned to me better than anyone expects.

3   I participate in group discussions and show that I care about the group goals. I complete the jobs assigned to me.

2   I participate in group discussions and show that I care about the group goals, but I do not do the jobs assigned to me.

1   I don't participate in group discussions or show that I care about the group goals; or I actually work against the goals.

B. I communicate well with the other group members.

4   I encourage good communication among the group members and try to make sure everyone shares their ideas. When I share my ideas, I show that I care about other people's feelings and ideas, and I encourage everyone in the group to do the same.

3   I participate in group discussions without being asked to. When I share my ideas, I show that I care about other people's feelings and ideas.

2   I participate in group discussions when I am asked to. When I share my ideas, I don't clearly show that I care about the feelings and ideas of others.

1   I do not participate in group discussions, even when asked to. I share ideas in a way that shows I don't really care about the feelings and ideas of others.

c. I help make sure the group works well together.

4   I encourage the group to evaluate how well we are working together. I try to get everyone involved in thinking of ways to make changes when we need to improve. When we decide to make changes. I try to make sure the changes help us work better together.

3   I participate in discussions of how well we are working together and help develop suggestions for changes when we need to improve. I work on making the changes that we agree to.

2   I participate in discussions of how well we are working together only when I am asked to, and I don't have ideas for ways to change. When we decide to change, I put little effort into making those changes.

1   I do not participate in discussing how well we are working together. When the group decides to change, I refuse to help work on the changes.

D.   I perform a variety of jobs in my group.

4   I perform many jobs in my group and do them all well.

3   I perform two jobs in my group and do both well.

2   I try to perform two jobs in my group but don't perform both well.

1   I don't even try to perform any more than one job in my group.

Habits of Mind Standards

A.   I am aware of my own thinking.

4   I describe in detail the steps of my thinking when I am solving a problem or doing other kinds of mental tasks. I explain in detail how thinking about my thinking helps me improve my work and how it helps me be a better learner.

3   I describe how I am thinking when I am solving a problem or doing other kinds of mental tasks. I explain how thinking about my thinking helps me learn and helps me improve my work.

2   I don't include very much information when I try to describe how I am thinking when I am solving a problem or doing other kinds of mental tasks. I explain only small benefits that can be gained from thinking about my own thinking.

1   I describe my thinking when I am solving a problem or doing other kinds of mental tasks, but my description is confusing. I do not describe how thinking about my thinking affects how I learn or do tasks.

B.   I plan carefully before I begin to work.

4   I set clear goals and describe each step I must take to achieve them. I make a detailed schedule for each step and closely follow the schedule.

3   I set clear goals and describe some steps I must take to achieve them. I make and use a schedule.

2   I begin working with only unclear goals. I describe few of the steps I must take to achieve my goals, and I make an incomplete schedule.

1   I begin working and just let things happen as they happen. I do not describe the steps I must take and I do not make a schedule.

C.   I am aware of available resources that could help me complete a task.

4   I describe in detail all the resources I think I might need before I start working on a task. I search for the resources available to me and, if something I need is not available, I describe other places I might get this help or information. I also predict what parts of the task will require the use of the most resources.

3   I list the most important resources I might need before I start working on a task. I review the resources that are available and describe other resources that I may have to find.

2   I begin working on a task and look for resources when I need them. This slows my work because I have to keep stopping to find the resources. When a resource is not available, I do not find other resources that might help.

1   As I am working on a task, I use resources only if they happen to be readily available. I do not use many resources that are available.

D.   I listen to and evaluate feedback to decide if I need to change my approach to a task.

4   I find and listen to information about how I am doing on a task. I change my approach when the feedback convinces me that what I'm doing isn't working. I seek advice from sources I know will give me good information about how my task is going. I study the information, no matter where it came from, and decide whether it is useful.

3   I listen to important information about how I am doing and decide if it will help me with my task. I change my approach to the task when the feedback convinces me that what I'm doing isn't working. I listen to advice and decide whether it is useful.

2   I listen to information about how I am doing only if the information is easy to get. If I don't like the source of the information, I don't listen. I don't like listening to advice from others.

1   I don't listen to most information that tells me how I am doing on a task. I refuse to accept information that tells me I should change my approach to the task.

E.   I evaluate how well I am doing.

4   I evaluate, in detail, how well I am doing by looking at my performance from my own point of view and by making sure I find out how others would evaluate my work. I describe the effect my work has right now and what effect it might have later. I explain how I can learn from my successes and my failures.

3   I evaluate how well I am doing and describe the effect my work has right now. I try to find out how others would evaluate my work. I explain how I can learn from what I do well on the task.

2   I evaluate how well I am doing, but I use only my own opinion. I don't describe the effects of my work and don't explain how I can learn from what I am doing.

1   I don't try to evaluate how well I am doing.

F.   I am accurate in my work.

4   I pay close attention to details. I check every useful source to make sure my work is completely accurate. when I find errors , I quickly correct the errors in a way that improves the value of the entire project.

3   I pay attention to details when I work. I check other sources to make sure my work is accurate. I find and correct major errors.

2   I try to pay attention to details in my work, but miss some important ideas. I check some sources to see if my work is accurate, but miss important places I should check. I miss important errors and fail to correct others.

1   I don't check to make sure my information is accurate. I make little effort to find and correct errors.

G.   I am clear in my work.

4   My work has no confusing parts.

3   The most important parts of my work are free of any confusion.

2   My work has some confusing parts that affect the whole.

1   My work has many confusing parts.

H.   I am open-minded.

4   I try to find ideas that are different from mine and evaluate them to decide if they make sense— even when the ideas are unusual.

3   When I come across ideas that are different from mine, I try to understand them.

2   I understand that other people have ideas different from mine, but I don't pay attention to these different ideas.

1   I believe my ideas are the only ideas worth listening to and I don't listen to people who have different ideas.

I. I avoid acting without thinking.

4   I evaluate a situation carefully and seek advice from other sources to decide whether I need more information before I act. When I decide more information is needed, I look for sources that might help and study them to find important information.

3   I evaluate a situation to decide if I need more information before I act. When I decide more information is needed, I look for that information.

2   I do only a quick evaluation of a situation to decide whether I need more information before I act. When I decide more information is needed, I look for some additional information only when it is easy to obtain.

1   I do not evaluate the situation to decide whether I need more information before I act.

J. I state my ideas or opinion if the issue or situation warrants it.

4   I state my ideas or opinion about an issue or situation when I believe I can shed light on the issue or situation. I give important information and provide a valuable and new way of looking at the issue or situation. I explain the important information that supports my ideas or opinions.

3   I state my ideas or opinion about an issue or situation when I believe I can give important support to a way of looking at the issue or situation. I explain the reasons for my ideas or opinion.

2   I state my ideas or opinion about an issue when comments are not really needed. My comments may simply repeat what has already been said or I may not clearly explain the reasons for my ideas or opinion.

1   I state my ideas or opinion in a way that is harmful to the situation. I cannot support my ideas or opinion.

K. I am sensitive to the feelings, knowledge, and abilities of others.

4   I evaluate situations to make sure I understand the feelings, knowledge, and abilities of others. I use this understanding when I communicate, and I encourage people to show respect for the different feelings, knowledge, and abilities of others.

3   I communicate well with people who have different feelings, knowledge, and abilities. I encourage people to show respect for the feelings, knowledge, and abilities of others.

2   I try but don't really understand the different feelings, knowledge, and abilities of others well enough to communicate effectively with them. I do little to encourage others to show respect for these differences.

1   I don't communicate well with people who have different feelings, knowledge, and abilities. In fact, I communicate that I don't care about their differences.

L.   I work hard on tasks even when the answers or solutions are difficult to find.

4   I show that I will not give up, no matter how difficult it is to find the answers or solutions. I evaluate how hard I am trying and I use a variety of techniques to keep myself on task.

3   I show that I don't give up when I am trying to find the answers or solutions. I keep myself on task.

2   I try to complete tasks when the answers or solutions are difficult, but I give up when I have to try too hard. I don't have good techniques for keeping myself on task.

1   I give up quickly on difficult tasks.

M.   I push myself to try things that I'm not sure I can do.

4   I look for tasks that I'm not sure I can do and stick with them until I've accomplished them or until I have learned all I can.

3   I try tasks that are given to me even when I'm not sure I can do them, and I stick with them until I've accomplished them or until I have learned all I can.

2   I try tasks that are given to me even when I'm not sure I can do them, but I give up before I accomplish them or before I have learned from them.

1   I avoid tasks that I'm not sure I can do.

N.   I create, trust, and use standards for evaluating my own work.

4   I create and trust standards for evaluating my own work. The standards I set are high enough to make me produce something of high quality. I make sure my final product meets those standards.

3   I create and trust standards for evaluating my own work. I make sure my final product meets those standards.

2   I create and trust standards for evaluating my own work, but I don't make sure my final product meets those standards.

1   I do not create standards for evaluating my own work.

O. **I find new ways of looking at situations that are different from the usual ways in which people look at them.**

4   I use time and resources creatively to find as many ways as possible to look at a situation. I evaluate these ways to see how useful they might be. My ways are very different from the ways of others, but often they are more useful.

3   I find a variety of ways of looking at a situation and evaluate how useful they are. Some of the ways I find are new and different.

2   I describe different ways of looking at a situation, but my ideas are common.

1   I look at a situation in only one way, and that way is one of the most common. I don't look further, even when it is clear that it would be helpful to do so.

9

Blank Forms

Throughout this book, we have shown samples of forms that may be used to support the assessment process. This chapter contains blank versions of those forms, which we encourage teachers to photocopy and use in their classrooms:

- Student Record Part I
- Student Record Part II
- Student Record Part III
- Task Evaluation Form
- Grade Book Form

Student Record
Part I

Student _____

CONTENT STANDARDS	Summary Validations				

Student Record
Part II

Student _____

COMPLEX THINKING	Summary Validations				
1. Effectively translates issues and situations into manageable tasks that have a clear purpose.					
2. Effectively uses a variety of complex reasoning strategies.					
INFORMATION PROCESSING	**Summary Validations**				
1. Effectively interprets and synthesizes information.					
2. Effectively uses a variety of information-gathering techniques and information resources.					
3. Accurately assesses the value of information.					
4. Recognizes where and how projects would benefit from additional information.					
EFFECTIVE COMMUNICATION	**Summary Validations**				
1. Expresses ideas clearly.					
2. Effectively communicates with diverse audiences.					
3. Effectively communicates in a variety of ways.					
4. Effectively communicates for a variety of purposes.					
5. Creates high-quality products.					

Student Record
Part III

Student _____

COLLABORATION/COOPERATION	Summary Validations				
1. Works toward the achievement of group goals.					
2. Demonstrates effective interpersonal skills.					
3. Contributes to group maintenance.					
4. Effectively performs a variety of roles in a group.					
HABITS OF MIND	**Summary Validations**				
1. Is aware of own thinking.					
2. Makes effective plans.					
3. Is aware of necessary resources.					
4. Is sensitive to feedback.					
5. Evaluates the effectiveness of own actions.					
6. Is accurate and seeks accuracy.					
7. Is clear and seeks clarity.					
8. Is open-minded.					
9. Restrains impulsivity.					
10. Takes a position when the situation warrants it.					
11. Is sensitive to the feelings and level of knowledge of others.					
12. Engages intensely in tasks even when answers or solutions are not immediately apparent.					
13. Pushes the limits of own knowledge and abilities.					
14. Generates, trusts, and maintains own standards of evaluation.					
15. Generates new ways of viewing a situation outside the boundaries of standard conventions.					

Task Evaluation Form

Student _____

STANDARDS	EVALUATION
	1 2 3 4
	1 2 3 4
	1 2 3 4
	1 2 3 4
	1 2 3 4
	1 2 3 4
	1 2 3 4
	1 2 3 4
	1 2 3 4
	1 2 3 4

Grade Book Form

STANDARD CATEGORY																			
STANDARD																			
ASSESSMENT KEY			Summary Validation				Summary Validation				Summary Validation				Summary Validation				Summary Validation
Student Names																			

About the Authors

Robert J. Marzano is Deputy Director of Training and Development, Mid-continent Regional Educational Laboratory, 2550 S. Parker Rd., Suite 500, Aurora, CO 80014.

Debra Pickering is Senior Program Associate, Mid-continent Regional Educational Laboratory, 2550 S. Parker Rd., Suite 500, Aurora, CO 80014.

Jay McTighe is Director, Maryland Assessment Consortium, c/o Frederick County Public Schools, 115 E. Church St., Frederick, MD 21701.

Acknowledgments

The authors thank John Kendall for his early work on the rubrics in this book. They also thank Jo Sue Whisler, Diane Paynter, and Fran Mayeski for their work on the performance task examples.